BOOK
PROPOSALS

The Essential Guide

Book Proposals – The Essential Guide is also available in accessible formats for people with any degree of sight loss. The large print edition and ebook (with accessibility features enabled) are available from Need2Know. Please let us know if there are any special features you require and we will do our best to accommodate your needs.

First published in Great Britain in 2000
Second edition 2011

Need2Know
Remus House
Coltsfoot Drive
Peterborough
PE2 9BF
Telephone 01733 898103
Fax 01733 313524
www.need2knowbooks.co.uk

Contents

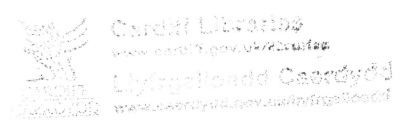

To Gordon Wells, friend and mentor

Introduction

Writing a book can be fun; it's hard work but fun. Especially if the synopsis is waiting to be written in the agony corner. No one wants to write one. But it won't go away. A synopsis is what editors want to see as part of your book proposal - a brilliant, professional synopsis that makes them eager to read your manuscript and hopefully buy it.

This How-To book should act as a carrot, the same way as buying that gorgeous size twelve dress will encourage you to diet. It will be your guide and mentor, your friend on the shelf. Every writer was once a beginner and, even after publication, we begin afresh with each new book.

Writing a synopsis does get easier! The first one is the killer. Completing your first synopsis will take away the fear. And once that is overcome, the next one does not seem quite such hard work. They are always going to be difficult, a chore, requiring hours of concentration. But if you are obsessed with writing and getting published, then you will do it.

Obsession is the one word that describes the truly professional writer. You keep on writing, working, slogging away at the word processor, whatever the hiccups and rejections.

Obsession comes in different forms. It means thinking like a writer all the time, even whilst watching a television documentary, going to a party, walking the dog . . . every facet of life is research. New people, faces, dialogue, clothes, impressions . . . plots and characters crowding into mind, waiting to be written into stories. Nothing is ever wasted. The mental filing cabinet is rattling away, storing scraps of information.

Research is only one aspect of the writing obsession. We enjoy making notes, talking to people, seeing new places - villages, castles, rivers, moors and mountains - taking an interest in absolutely everything. Nothing is boring. Life is never boring. Everything is waiting to be written about. We are the only people who can get something out of standing in a supermarket queue.

No day is complete without writing, be it on a typewriter, keyboard or in longhand. Pens still work. I once wrote a whole short story on a brown paper bag and it was published. A day without a single word written is a day wasted that can never be recovered. Time passes so quickly. My idea of hell would be if St Peter handed me a typewriter but said they were clean out of paper.

I started writing seriously at the age of nine. My father gave me a second-hand Imperial typewriter to ease the boredom of a bad case of measles. I sat up in bed, thrilled beyond words and, covered in spots, began to type with two fingers. I wrote stories, produced a magazine, began a novel. (Instead of paying attention in class.)

I became a cub reporter on a South London newspaper with the ambition of learning how to write. My chief reporter, the legendary Vic Davis, was ruthless with my work. I was given all the worst jobs but I gritted my teeth and eventually became one of the first women chief reporters, certainly the youngest, and possibly the only pregnant one.

'A day without a single word written is a day wasted that can never be recovered.'

Short stories were my first love and still are. But then, to my amazement, an encouraging editor, James Law, told me that a book is a series of short stories joined together and only marginally frightening if viewed as such. And there's no set age for writing. Writers don't grow old, they merely mature like a good brandy.

So I'm guessing that you may be:

- A complete beginner, writing your first book, hoping to ignore the need for a synopsis.

- A writer with a few isolated successes who knows that a good synopsis might open a few more doors.

- A moderately successful author who is determined that the next one is going to be the big one, and who has the synopsis mentally planned but unwritten.

Being able to write a brilliant synopsis could make all the difference. It is a discipline that can be learned. Don't worry too much because it is possible for a new writer to take the general concept on board. But it's a hard day's work so get a good night's sleep. Put on some favourite music, pour yourself a glass of chilled wine, and switch on your word processor

This time you are really going to write a synopsis.

Choosing the right time

There are no rules about when to write a synopsis. It could be before you've written a word of your book, when you are halfway through or when you've nearly finished. The essential moment is before you first approach an agent or a publisher, or both.

It is permitted to be seeking an agent and a publisher at the same time. If you get a publisher, then an agent will be delighted to take you on. If you get an agent first, then they will take over offering your manuscript.

Agents and publishers are incredibly busy people because so many of us want to write and be published. Their postman arrives every morning, staggering under the weight of fresh manuscripts. I've seen the slush piles on the floor of their offices, all quivering with hope. The staff are faced with falling over bulky piles of unread manuscripts every time they open a door. Imagine having to plough through all those millions of words. Imagine carrying them home, straphanging on the underground . . .

But a synopsis and the first couple of chapters is a more manageable possibility. It's small, it's portable, it can be taken home, read on the train. And it tells the editorial reader all that he wants to know. He asks himself four questions:

- Is there a story here that I like?

- Can this writer write?

- Is there enough material for a whole book?

- Would the book sell?

A good synopsis can sell a book. You are going to give it your best shot. It's the only one you've got unless you are related to the publisher, or are his daughter's best friend.

Different treatments

There are several different types of synopsis. This book will detail the sixteen-step treatment which can be used for any genre of novel; romance, saga, middle of the road, or literary.

Crime, thrillers, any kind of whodunnit require a manifold approach, an extra dimension. Basically the same, but with an important structural difference.

Non-fiction, again, needs a specialised approach, selling the contents, not a story. And the synopsis for radio and TV is completely different. If your ambition is to reach the small screen, then knowing how to produce an idea synopsis is vital.

The spark

'It's the idea that counts, makes the blood tingle, explodes in your mind like a thousand shooting stars.'

It's a lovely feeling, getting the idea for a story. The long months of work ahead are not daunting. It's the idea that counts, makes the blood tingle, explodes in your mind like a thousand shooting stars. Savour that moment. It's a gift from the patron saint of good ideas, St Fantasticus. Nothing will feel that good again until you type those magic words 'the end'.

Every conception is different. A different fictional lover . . . some come from a beginning, another from an ending, perhaps a character or a place, anything that sets the mind spinning and ideas spilling over. But it has to be a strong idea. Don't stop to think what has started your story. Just get going.

Revision and polishing

These are the writer's secret weapon. Writers who say that they don't revise are surely missing moments of sheer pleasure. I can think of no greater feeling of accomplishment than honing through work, making it tighter, cleaner, better writing, finding the odd touch of a rainbow suddenly lifting the prose.

You've done the slog of getting out a first draft. It is sitting on your knee, a satisfying wedge of paper. Now comes the best part. Revising is a joy. Agonising over even one word is stirring the grey cells to work for you. Make them work. (Don't use your mobile phone unless it's an emergency.) Every grey cell is vital to your intellect. They should not be squandered.

Polishing is an absorbing delight that can be done anywhere, on the train, in the garden, on the beach. It's still working . . . oh yes, it's work indeed of the highest calibre. Every unnecessary word is deleted. Your writing is purged of excesses, made pure, made clean. Adjectives and adverbs are eliminated, dialogue sharpened. *Hone, sharpen, whittle and polish.* This is your chance to add a touch of poetry, paint a different picture.

Dedication

And this dedication applies to the writing of a synopsis, even a one-page or two-page synopsis - those important but simple two-line paragraphs that have to spell out your story so vividly that an editor wants to read more.

It's a herculean task, make no mistake. Writers have to go into a dedicated homework-mode. There's no other word for it. It's doing your homework that brings home the bacon. (*Cut!* No cliches here, please. We're proper writers.)

'Hone, sharpen, whittle and polish.'

Chapter One

The Dreaded Synopsis

'Synopsis' is a peculiar word. It's late Latin from the Greek 'sunopsis'. It sounds like an illness, something vaguely septic; and the sight of it frequently brings on symptoms of despair and wretchedness in writers. My dictionary says:

Synopsis -

a condensation or brief review of a subject, a summary.

If you think of 'opsis' as meaning a view then the word is not nearly so alarming. The prefix 'syn' means with, together or a fusion. A fusion of a view is pleasant, even poetic, a misty sunlit afternoon. Your fusion of your view makes it personal to your story. If Roget's Thesaurus is permanently attached to your right hand, then you will already know that he gives three further meanings:

- Arrangement.
- List.
- Compendium.

Now these meanings are not alarming. We make arrangements, lists and compendiums every day. Well, perhaps not compendiums but that only means a book of useful items. Your synopsis is going to be a mini book of very useful information.

A fusion of a view is pleasant, even poetic, a misty sunlit afternoon.

Targets to remember

- Your synopsis should be stunning and professional.
- The time and care spent on it will bring its own reward.
- The writing of your synopsis should be of equal worth to the writing of your whole book.

Still you may ask: what is a synopsis? A synopsis shows the contents and flavour of a novel in a brief form. It sounds simple but it isn't. To produce a good synopsis means concentrated, sweat on the brow stuff. It could be compared to a short narrative story.

Why is it important? Because if you don't know what your book is about, how is an editor able to tell if they could sell it or you can write it?

Why is it important to get it right? A poor synopsis will sabotage your novel before the first chapter even gets a first reading.

By now the thought of beginning a synopsis should be less alarming. This is by making it workable, almost human, taming the dragon, it need no longer be one of the chores that writers put off doing, like a tax return.

The three basic functions of a synopsis are:

- As a visible aid for the writer.
- To attract the interest of an editor in your work.
- And, thirdly, to eventually sell your book.

'Why is it important to get it right? A poor synopsis will sabotage your novel before the first chapter even gets a first reading.'

Your own personal opsis

This amazing story idea that you have germinating and growing in your mind needs sorting out into some sort of order before you start writing, and a synopsis is one way to do it. You must have a clear idea what your book is about and where it is going to go. It helps you decide whether you really do have a story and whether there is enough plot to fill an approximate number of pages. It fixes its identity and sets the boundaries.

Firstly, write everything down that comes into your mind about this new story . . . scenes, high points and lows, bits of dialogue, characters . . . all the odds and ends, a fictional collage of your book. You could be organised and use a notebook. You could scribble on old envelopes, saving trees. But get everything down that you know about your novel and put it all in one place . . . a file, a cereal box, the cat's basket, anywhere, as long as you know where it is.

Authors are allowed to be eccentric. Clutter seems to go with writing. But it won't work if your novel is strewn all over the house and you spend precious hours searching for one vital piece of paper.

Your sales pitch

Your synopsis is a sales pitch, your TV commercial. You have only got so many soundbites, so many lines, with which to sell your book. Make every second of an editor's reading time work for you.

A synopsis is quite different from an outline, which is a more detailed, chapter-by-chapter blueprint that charts the progress of a plot, graphs the highs and lows, reminds you of easily forgotten sub-plots and loose ends. An outline is your day-to-day work manual, your personal route map, for your eyes only.

'Your synopsis isn't cast in concrete.'

The synopsis and an outline are often confused. A synopsis is written in narrative form; an outline is a chart showing the progress of your plot. You would not send a progress chart to an editor - this is your visual prop and guide.

A crime synopsis has an element of charting, but it is charting clues, red herrings, twists and turns.

At the same time, there is no rule that says you have to keep to your synopsis. It isn't cast in concrete. It isn't a straitjacket. If, much later, you or your characters dictate a different twist or turn, then follow it, as long as the main theme stays the same and the leading characters still hold the floor. A contemporary romance that suddenly turns into science fiction or horror gothic has lost its identity; a minor character that takes over and ousts the hero has to be brought under control.

Attracting an editor

The prime reason for writing a synopsis is to attract an editor's attention. In these days, the slush piles of unsolicited manuscripts are enough to send overworked editors jumping off the roof of the Dome. It makes sense to send in a book proposal or partial, not a complete manuscript.

A book proposal, or partial, is normally the first two or three chapters, a synopsis and a brief letter of personal introduction. The synopsis tells an editor several things about you and your book:

- Whether you have a story there.
- Whether it is different, unique, has some special quality.
- Whether you know what you are doing and where you are going.
- Whether you can sustain the story and if there is enough plot for the proposed length.
- Whether the novel slots into one of their categories.
- Whether they have already published something similar.

An editor does not need the complete manuscript of your novel in order to assess these points. Also, at this stage, an editor can make helpful suggestions, spot weaknesses, guide your work towards publication.

An editor's interest is invaluable, and any advice is worth thinking about even if you do not agree or follow it to the letter.

It gives an editor a chance to say if the plot is a bit thin, if she likes the characters, if there are too many, if a major scene doesn't work. She will also comment on the overall doom and gloom aspect of your story, whether there is sufficient content for an uplifting or satisfactory ending.

If an editor suggests changes, it is less frustrating to do this before you have progressed too far into the book. Serious writers don't ride high horses.

'A book proposal, or partial, is normally the first two or three chapters, a synopsis and a brief letter of personal introduction.'

Unless you have a track record, editors rarely commission fiction on the strength of a synopsis. But they can and do express an interest, and that's important and worth having. Non-fiction is the exception to this rule. A non-fiction work can be commissioned on a more detailed chapter-by-chapter synopsis, sample chapter and known writing ability.

On a practical side, sending a partial saves a lot of time and money. The cost of sending a heavy manuscript, with return postage, can be a big outlay. Emailing your submission is even cheaper and quicker, but check first whether the agent/publisher will accept emailed manuscripts. If the email address includes the recipient's name then the right person will read it.

There are many writers who never work with a synopsis and would not dream of producing one. They say it kills the story for them. They have no clear idea of where their story is going. They begin with a germ that grows along with their characters and takes on a life of its own. If this is the way you prefer to work, then go ahead. Do what works for you.

Other writers prefer to finish the whole novel and then submit a partial with a synopsis. The problem with this method is that when the whole book is before you in cleanly typed glory, it can be difficult trying to decide which are the major scenes. You get side-tracked by the delicious bits and pieces that you cannot resist including in the synopsis to show editors how clever you have been.

Tense and timing

A synopsis is written in the present tense. The past tense is used for flash-backs. When you have sent off your book proposal or partial, don't sit back and think oh good, now I can have a month off, go fishing. Carry on writing. Don't stop the creative flow. If you wait - possibly six weeks - for a reply, it might be hard work getting back into your story.

Length

Irving Wallace's synopsis for his book 'The Prize' was 40 pages long. It is a complicated book. I suggest as a rough guide that one page of synopsis is about right for every 20,000 words of a planned novel. So a five-page synopsis should cover a 100,000 word novel. Again, there are no rules, but make your synopsis shorter rather than longer.

A Mills & Boon synopsis is even shorter. They prefer one or two pages but only after they have approved an initial letter briefly outlining the story. Now, that's difficult. You have to encapsulate your plot into a few arresting paragraphs.

I always hated writing synopses with the result that they were dreadful. I simply did not recognise what to put in them and wrote aimlessly in circles, padding out the prose with verbosity. No wonder they were sent back. Here is an exaggerated example of a synopsis that doesn't work.

The requirement today is becoming shorter and shorter. If you can get everything on to one page, single-spacing, well done. My current 100,000 word saga has a two-page synopsis.

'The requirement today is becoming shorter and shorter. If you can get everything on to one page, single-spacing, well done.'

A Pathetic Synopsis

This story (no title) is about a man and a woman (no names) who meet on the fabulous cosmopolitan (jargon) ski-slopes of Austria (no detail). Wonderful background of sparkling snow, parties, etc (what does etc mean?). They are both successful (really?) but the hero is very wealthy indeed (how come?). They fall in love (when?) but he has a former girl-friend (oh, yes), a blue-eyed blonde bombshell (cliché) who makes a lot of trouble (what sort?) and the heroine gets very upset (how much?) and rushes home to England in tears. All is lost and it becomes a hopeless patchwork of despair (padding). Eventually (how long?) they meet again (where?) and soon realise that they love each other madly (how are they sure?) and there is a happy ever after ending (what kind of happy ending?).

This synopsis does not work on any level. No editor is going to reach for the phone. The author has not thought through the story, does not know the characters, and I doubt if she will ever write it.

When I began to write for Mills & Boon, I found it was essential to submit a good synopsis with each new story idea put forward. I had to learn how to do it professionally if I wanted my editor to be interested in my next book. A synopsis is a sales tool. It has selling power. If I wanted to sell my next book, then it was up to me to produce a synopsis that was concise, bright, intriguing and of the highest possible writing standard.

I was determined to learn how to do it. Make or break time was staring at me from the screen.

Step-by-step synopsis

After several sleepless weeks, I had broken down the requirements of an average fictional synopsis into sixteen steps, the last four being optional.

These four are my extras which I like to put in. They are my individual touches - but you are welcome to use them, or think up some new ingredients of your own. It's like baking a cake. You can improvise. But here is the basic recipe:

The sixteen steps

1. The setting and *title*. Where and when the action takes place. This is one straight forward sentence saying where the story is set and when in time.

2. The hero and heroine or main characters. Introduce your main characters by name, age, professional background, making them sound special and alive. Add any secondary character who has an important role in the plot. Two paragraphs is enough.

3. Add a few details of family background, wealth, status, history. One concise paragraph should be adequate.

4. The main critical situation at the opening of your novel. Briefly describe the dynamic thrust of your story in a single sentence.

5. Now set the mood and tone of the piece. Try to create the *atmosphere* of your story in one sentence.

6. That special ingredient. If your story has something special or *unique* about it, say so in another sentence. And keep plugging the *title*.

7. The conflict and drama of the story. Get your teeth into this one but keep it to one strong and powerful paragraph. Quality writing always.

I expect you have realised by now that these seven points are the foundation of your novel and most of them will be the substance of your initial two chapters.

So, you may ask: why put this information in the synopsis if most of it is contained in the first two chapters? Answer: an editor gets the feel of the whole book from the synopsis; the sample chapters demonstrate your ability to write and follow a synopsis. She'll spot immediately if they don't tally and you have gone wildly off course.

The first two chapters of crime or thrillers need an extra dimension. They have to intrigue, hint at what is to come, set the crime scene, introduce the sleuth, murderer or the victim, establish the forward-moving problem or mystery.

'These seven points are the foundation of your novel.'

Now back to those sixteen steps:

8. Major scenes. Mention *title* again. This is the time to list several of the most important scenes - not every scene in the book - tasters of what the reader can expect to enjoy. A bit like programme notes for an evening's television. Two paragraphs will do justice to this step.

9. The forwards and backwards movement of the story as endured by the characters. What are the ups and downs, the positive and the negative side of the drama? And especially that darkest moment and how the main character is affected. An emotional route-map in a single paragraph. Quite a tall order.

10. The decision-making scene. Now we are nearing the end. What is the scene that changes everything? It's crucial that the turning point is clearly sign-posted in a sentence.

11. The important final scene. The climax. The finale. A crescendo of invention in a dramatic paragraph.

12. A brief conclusion. Wrap it up in a good, satisfying sentence.

These twelve steps will tell an editor everything she needs to know about your story. (70% of publishing staff are female.) It will also tell her a lot about you, so it pays to take trouble and to write it to the very best of your ability. Don't worry if steps 5 and 9 are too difficult to summarise. They are difficult. If in doubt, leave out. Make the synopsis steps work for you.

And no secrets please. The editor will not be amused if you hint coyly that there is a brilliant twist ending, but you aren't going to tell anyone yet. By all means save small surprises to amaze your editor when she reads the complete manuscript, but the end of the story should be clearly stated in your synopsis. Okay, the butler did it. Trust her, the editor won't tell a soul.

Lastly use strong words, strong verbs. Make everything exciting and dramatic. Even that pathetic synopsis had the nameless heroine *rushing* home to England, not merely going or travelling.

The optional four

These are my four optional steps. I like to believe these add an extra dimension.

'Use strong words, strong verbs.'

13. A single line of dialogue from the heroine or main character. They bring her to life. They should be words which really show her character and style and the way she talks. Make it vivid. You've only got this one chance for her to speak.

14. Example of dialogue from the hero or another character. This should also show his character and make him come striding off the paper. Let the editor hear his voice, preferably with a line that is pertinent to the plot.

15. Example of emotional or sensuous writing, if this is relevant to your story. Show that you can write something really romantic, full of emotion or sexual promise. Or a line that's chilling or exciting if it's a thriller. Again this is a taster, showing off your writing skill.

16. Putting in the poetry, painting a picture. This is a chance to add - only a few words please, a single phrase at the most - something visual and poetic that gives your synopsis that extra dimension. Be on that moorland, smell that sea, hear those birds. Add a brush of poetry.

These four steps can be put into your synopsis at any point, wherever it seems a natural addition. You might add an example of dialogue after step 4 (main critical situation) and another after step 7 (conflict and drama). An example of emotional or sensuous writing might fit in after your paragraph of major scenes. As for that touch of poetry, the rainbow chasing your mind . . . it can go in anywhere.

Peter Mark Roget was an English physician who wrote his *Thesaurus of English Words and Phrases* in 1852 when he had retired. He was already 73 years old and lived another 17 years. When I reach that great writers' conference in the sky, I hope to meet him. I should like to thank him for producing an invaluable writers' bible. When I recorded the programme *Desert Island Discs* in the Falklands, Roget was my choice of book to take along to that treeless sweep of mined and booby-trapped white sand.

'Hello Dr Roget,' I'll say to him. 'It's a wonderful book. Did you have to submit a synopsis?'

'A synopsis?' he'll say thoughtfully. 'Arrangement, list, compendium? Graduation, classification, order, digest? Catalogue, inventory, schedule? Precis, analysis, summary?'

'In a nutshell, dear Peter,' I'll agree. 'In a nutshell.'

Summing Up

- Do I know my story inside out?
- Have I planned the sixteen steps?
- Am I using strong words?
- Have I kept to the required length?
- Cut, cut and cut again.
- Treat: a cup of coffee and digestive biscuit!

Chapter Two
Let's Write A Synopsis

By now you may feel confident enough to try writing a synopsis of your own. This is best written in longhand first on a big pad of paper with plenty of room allowed for alterations and additions. Rule off a left-hand margin and at intervals put a word or two that will remind you of the sixteen suggested steps.

The headings could be:

- 1. Setting.
- 2. Main characters.
- 3. Background.
- 4. Critical situation.
- 5. Mood.
- 6. Special ingredient.
- 7. Conflict.
- 8. Major scenes.
- 9. Ups and downs.
- I0. Decision.
- 11. Finale.
- 12. Conclusion.
- plus 13. Dialogue (f).
- 14. Dialogue (m).
- 15. Sensuality.
- and 16. Poetry.

Work slowly and methodically, one paragraph at a time. Simplify and condense the story-line. Tighten every sentence.

When you come to type it up (single-spacing) begin with a heading that gives relevent information. Also, put your address at the top of the first page and the expected length of the novel. Like this:

Your address

The Title

planned length, say: 70,000 words/10 chapters

a romance/thriller/murder mystery (whatever)

by

Your writing name

> 'Work slowly and methodically, one paragraph at a time.'

Then start typing your synopsis, set out in normal paragraphs. No need to invent a fancy layout.

A sample synopsis

This is the final synopsis of my book called *Daughter of Tor*, showing how I used the sixteen steps to give the clearest possible analysis of the plot. It went through three drafts before it was ready to send off.

My address

Daughter of Tor

10 chapters/50-55,000 words

a contemporary romance

by

Stella Whitelaw

Synopsis

- 1. This modern day romance erupts during the summer term at Belling Hills, an expensive girls' boarding school in South Devon, near Dartmoor and the beautiful South Devon coast.

(Note: deliberate use of verb 'erupt'; also I have stated the duration of the story as being a summer term.)

- 2. Sister Troy Kingsbury is the resident sister at the school's medical centre, a tall, sensitive woman in her late twenties, recovering from a traumatic divorce. The headmistress, Grace Howard, has a brother, Jonathan Howard, who at 36 sees his career as an orthopaedic surgeon virtually at an end.

(Thumb-nail sketches. Note: there's very little about appearance; it's not necessary at this stage unless it is crucial to story, i.e. someone is blind. The hardest character to write about is a deaf person. Think about it.)

- 3. The repossession of her married home caused Troy severe anguish after her divorce. Living in the Coastguard's Cottage on the school estate is helping to restore her confidence, when Jonathan arrives to convalesce after a helicopter accident in which the nerves of his hands have been severed.

(Note: no long rigmarole. Plain facts stated, using strong words.)

- 4. The conflict arises from Troy's indignation and distress at being turned out of her beloved cottage for a man, a top medical man, who gives every indication that he's about to interfere with the way she runs the medical centre at the school.

(Note: this gives strong clues about their characters . . . Troy's distrust of men; Jonathan's natural arrogance.)

- 5. The tone of *Daughter of Tor* is the paradox of raging calm; their raging and passionate emotions against the calming background of sea, hills and cliffs, with nature reflecting their changing moods.

(Note: I'm hoping this is going to work. Raging Calm is an alternative title - there is no copyright in titles and it has been used before by Stan Barstow, but it's almost perfect for my story.)

6. Two emerging issues are the recognition of the subtle physical and emotional signs that could mean a child is being abused, and the importance of child bereavement therapy which is often ignored.

(Note: this says that the story is not only a complicated, sensual romance . . . there are also important and serious social issues.)

7. Troy has to fight Jonathan on several levels; his interference in her job, his apathy about ever being fit to operate, and her growing attraction to him when she thought such physical feelings had gone forever. They cross swords at every meeting, their angry exchanges heightened by hidden emotions.

(Note: it would be wrong to detail all these small scenes even if you are longing to share the exciting dialogue you have already heard in your head. Write them down somewhere else.)

> 'It would be wrong to detail all these small scenes even if you are longing to share the exciting dialogue you have already heard in your head.'

8. Major medical scenes include a girl pupil hit on the head during games; a boy saved from drowning; a distressed runaway and her forceful exam-mad parents; a pupil whose mother dies unexpectedly; an asthmatic girl locking herself in a lavatory to smoke and Jonathan climbing up to rescue her; a local farmer seriously gored by a bull.

(Note: since this story has a medical background, the chief medical scenes are detailed. An editor might say no to some illnesses or operations, AIDS or abortion, for instance.)

The emotional tangle grows as Troy finds herself falling in love with Jonathan, and the arrival of his awkward 13-year-old daughter, Amanda, does nothing to help. Troy discovers his wife left him years ago and has since died. He is like another lost child for all his skill and medical reputation. She longs to tell him that she cares, but he recoils from her tenderness.

(Note: new twist introduced, new character.)

9. When Troy and Jonathan are walking the spectacular South Devon coastal path, or exploring the steeply stepped streets of Dartmouth, they find much to enjoy in each other's company. Troy tries to help him exercise his fingers, keyboard typing, playing the piano. But the moment they get too close, Jonathan backs off, leaving Troy humiliated that she has allowed her

emotions to show and her physical desire to be aroused. He tells her that he will never trust a woman again, that she should forget him; he has no intention of ever allowing another woman into his life.

- Meanwhile the threads of the other storylines are woven into the romance; Troy becomes alerted to a girl's unconscious calls for help; the bereavement therapy shows positive results and the two girls, Lucy and Sarah, respond to Troy's warm-hearted attention, eventually becoming friends.

(Note: we are now pulling the threads together.)

- 10. The scene which changes the situation is when Jonathan is forced to do an emergency operation on the gored farmer who may die from loss of blood. With the return of his confidence and the mobility of his fingers, he realises that his career is all important again, but hesitates to tell Troy, knowing it will make her unhappy. He returns abruptly to London, without even saying goodbye, leaving Troy desolate and heartbroken.

(Note: this is called the darkest moment.)

- 11. A freak autumn storm blows up high tides; people are injured by falling trees and in fishing boat accidents. Troy is too busy tending casualties at Loop Cove to think of her cottage, standing so close to the cliff's edge. But Jonathan drives down overnight from London, knowing she might be in danger, just as the garden of the Coastguard's Cottage disappears in a landslide. He saves her from death as the rear wall of the cottage plunges over the cliff.

(Note: be brief, be dramatic.)

- 12. They realise that they love each other and cannot live apart. They work out how this can be made possible, with a new life for Amanda and hope for the other two girls in the story.

(Note: tie up the loose ends quickly.)

The last four optional pieces can be inserted anywhere or omitted altogether. In your synopsis, you are the boss. I like to put them in, if it seems natural and adds texture to the synopsis. So, four more steps and it's done.

- 13. 'I hope you will recognise that I'm in charge of the medical health of these girls and I won't stand for any interference on your part,' says Troy. 'You may be a very important surgeon in London, but down here, you're just the man living uninvited in my cottage.' (Very brisk.)

(Note: you can hear her voice and she states the conflict situation again.)

- 14. 'Saved him? Yes, I suppose I did save the boy because I happen to be capable of blowing oxygen into his lungs. But what about those patients, young and old, who have little or no future beyond pain and immobility and all because of me, because of my hands?' Jonathan's face pales, his voice numb with anguish. 'What use is a surgeon who can't hold a knife steady? I'm useless.'

(Note: his voice is clear and his anguish over his injured hands apparent.)

- 15. He takes her face in his hands, tracing her skin with gentle fingers, catching his breath sharply as she moves closer. Their mouths touch, tentatively at first, tasting a new, tantalising taste, both suddenly shaken by an impatience that catches them unawares. 'Who taught you to kiss like this?' he asks. 'You did,' she whispers.

(Note: just enough to show that you can write a tender love scene.)

- 16. Bold and silent hills . . . changing sea songs . . . wind-tangled skeins . . . rags of clouds . . . silken skin . . . poppy bruised . . . icepick thoughts . . . daisies umbrellaed with dew . . . sheared cliffs . . .

(Note: a phrase, nothing more, somewhere.)

That's my synopsis for *Daughter of Tor*. (The paragraphs are numbered as a step-by-step guide for you. Don't number your synopsis.) It's not *Gone with the Wind* but it does say a lot about *Daughter of Tor* and leaves me free to expand in any way that I want. I'm not tied to anything and I'm going to enjoy writing it. I can feel the scenes fairly leaping off the page. Sparkle and spontaneity can have their way. And they probably will.

Freedom

As Michael Legat says in his book *Plotting the Novel (Hale)*, 'Like most self-imposed disciplines, that of working to a synopsis becomes a freedom.' How true.

'As Michael Legat says, "Like most self-imposed disciplines, that of working to a synopsis becomes a freedom."'

Need2Know

Don't be put off by the thought of the hard work that goes into writing a synopsis. It is going to save you time and trouble eventually. It becomes a friend at hand, and because you have *done it*, you are now free to write.

Katherine Anne Porter wrote: 'Courage is the first essential'. And Humpty Dumpty says, 'When it comes to words, it's a matter of who's to be master, that's all.'

Summing Up

- Keep mentioning the *title*.
- Name characters clearly.
- Select the best examples of dialogue.
- Have you used the present tense throughout?
- Is the font and layout plain?
- Treat: a good glass of wine!

Chapter Three

The Outline

An outline is a chapter-by-chapter breakdown of your novel. Scott Fitzgerald's method was to have a separate sheet of paper for each chapter and pin them round the walls like washing. I prefer to use a large piece of cardboard - from a shirt package is ideal - or a large sheet of paper. I want to be able to see the entire book in scenes at a glance. It gives me a sense of balance, a sense of purpose.

Why is an outline helpful?

It is your personal route-map that will take you from the opening paragraph to when, exhausted and parched, eventually you type the word end. It is a framework on which to plot the scenes in each chapter so that the action is well paced, to graph the high and low points in the story, to show you where to plant clues and red herrings.

It also enables you to check whether the actions and motivations of characters stay within believability.

Time spent on plotting an outline is time saved later. You may sit down at your desk ready to work after an unforeseen interruption, with your train of thought broken if not severed. Where were you in the story when you last worked? You read what you last wrote, revising and polishing as you read but you are lost. You seem to have washed inspiration down the plughole when you shampooed your hair.

But help is at hand. A glance at the outline for the current chapter and suddenly you know exactly what is the next move in the story whether it's major or minor. Write yourself in with a little narrative or linking dialogue, even a few lines about the weather . . . and you are back in harness.

'It is your personal route-map that will take you from the opening paragraph to when, exhausted and parched, eventually you type the word end.'

Starting to make an outline

Take the said large sheet of cardboard or paper, a ruler, pen or coloured felt tips if you are into colour:

- Divide the sheet into equal sections according to the number of proposed chapters.
- Label each space chapter 1, chapter 2 etc.

Before you go any further, re-read your own synopsis of the book. Note this account of your story and begin the mental pacing. Where exactly in the book is this scene going to happen, that confrontation take place?

- Briefly write in the details of the initial two chapters. You should sail through these two since you are already writing them.
- Don't let precious ideas slip away like smoke signals. Have your outline at hand always, on your desk, by the telephone, next to the kettle, anywhere that's visible and accessible. Work on it all the time.

'You will soon develop your own graphics and shorthand.'

Now you can start playing with your coloured felt tips if you want to. Perhaps blue for background narrative, orange for major scenes, black for troughs of despair and red for romance.

My own system is less hi-tech. I prefer to use ordinary pens, some black, some blue. Important scenes are underlined. Major scenes are in capital letters. Love scenes are a square with L/S written inside (is this Freudian?). Some details are circled. There's also wavy underlining which means 'build on this'. Question marks query items I'm not sure about.

You will soon develop your own graphics and shorthand.

- Space out the major scenes. A reader will soon lose interest if everything happens in chapter 2.
- Chart the highs and lows of emotion, conflict and drama, including the darkest moment. This kind of graph goes up and down like a temperature chart, the darkest moment coming at about two-thirds through. A roller-coaster ride with your heroine strapped into the front seat.
- If romance figures strongly in your story, then it's sensible to make some decisions in advance. It does make sense to decide early on when your

major love scenes may be and plot the setting, or you may find they take place in a broom cupboard or halfway down the M1. The reader will feel cheated if there are two love scenes in chapter 3 and nothing more till a final breathless clinch on page 186. And don't forget the URST (Unresolved Sexual Tension). Romances live on a diet of URST.

How to change your outline

You can change your outline anytime. A synopsis is not a contract which you dare not alter, nor is your outline. Characters often take over and change the direction of a story, or initiate better scenes than the ones you first thought of. It's OK to change things.

Take a red pen and draw arrows. If a major scene plotted for chapter 7 works better in chapter 4, then arrow it straight to its new home. If chapter 4 then overruns, move the unwritten scenes onto the next chapter with smaller arrows.

You may then find that chapter 7 is light without a major scene. If chapter 4 has overrun, this is going to shift several scenes forward and the overrun of chapter 6 will fill chapter 7.

Stories have a way of self-expanding, like popcorn exploding in a pan. You may be in despair at the beginning but by the time you are halfway into your novel, you will have so much material you may have arrows going round to the back of the board.

'Stories have a way of self-expanding, like popcorn exploding in a pan.'

Scaffolding, symphonies and stakes

If preparing an outline totally eludes you, then perhaps you haven't really thought your story through.

Authors often see their novel projected in their minds like scenes on television, the cameras rolling, actors and actresses in place, almost word-perfect. I switch on when I'm swimming or walking; I carry my own personal, waterproof TV. If this is new to you then set aside a particular space every day for thinking time - in the bath, waiting for a train, with your morning cuppa.

Don't feel guilty. Thinking time is still working time. As Lord Ted Willis's family put it: 'Dad's writing in his head.'

Every line you write has invisible scaffolding. It's the thinking time before you put a word on paper. And the more scaffolding, the stronger your story.

Authors who never plan a synopsis, never plot an outline, still go through the thinking process. They know their characters so well that they hardly need to wonder what is going to happen next. But to strike a musical note - a story is like a symphony. The instrumentalists are the ingredients of your novel and you are the conductor holding them together. But where would they be without a score? Everyone would be playing their own thing. The outline is my score.

If you don't know how to get started, ask yourself these questions:

- Do I really care about this story?

- Have I got a theme?

- Is it a personal indulgence?

- What is this story about?

- What is at stake?

- Is this story going anywhere?

Be honest with yourself. People often say, 'Oh, I could write a fantastic book about what my father did in the war.' No, they couldn't. They just think they could. And I'm not simply talking about the dedication, the self-discipline, the hours of hard work that would be required. What they have in mind is not professionally written work but an indulgence.

So do you care about this story? Are you obsessed with it? Are your thoughts constantly flying to it when you should be concentrating on other things, i.e. mundane work? Do you dream about it? Are the characters beginning to talk to you, give themselves names, likes and dislikes, occupations? Do you watch television and realise that you haven't taken in a single word? Do you passionately want to write this story?

Need2Know

Do you care enough? If your answers are vaguely no, then the story isn't for you. There must be a burning passion behind every piece of writing. I ache to write my short stories; they consume me with an intensity of longing to write them. I am passionate about writing.

A theme can be very simple. It doesn't have to be the stuff of an Honours degree. It is the reason behind the plot, an attitude. Rejection, insecurity, revenge, loneliness, loss of self-image, grieving, struggles, manipulation, hunger, mid-life crisis, finding oneself, hypocrisy . . . it's the unifying idea that develops throughout a story. A person's need . . . the need to be loved, to belong, to be successful.

There are endless themes. Read today's news stories and decide the underlying theme of each story. They will surprise you. To go back to that symphony score, the theme is the melody.

Distance yourself

Self-indulgence is a deadly trap for the writer. There may be a personal story you're desperate to write because it satisfies some inner need. You've always wanted to write about how your interfering neighbours get their comeuppance, or your impossible boss suffers some horrible grizzly end. There may be a very big novel there, but are you quite sure that this fantasising isn't going to be boring for the reader? Write it by all means, if it gets these repressed feelings off your chest, but don't expect anyone to publish it.

You need to distance yourself. If you take a personal experience, use that as a basis and develop it into a work of fiction. Don't write about your traumatic divorce. Let one of your characters go through a traumatic divorce. That firsthand knowledge will make it highly readable.

Sometimes a very personal story needs to be written as self-therapy. I lost a baby and couldn't stop grieving. I wrote it out, the story was published and the process seemed to go full circle with a new baby.

'There are endless themes. Read today's news stories and decide the underlying theme of each story. They will surprise you.'

Stake

Where the story is going is a verb. It becomes a non-plot when there is no movement and nothing much happens. If your story is static; it's not going anywhere. It needs a fast injection of drama, conflict, of dynamic major scenes and a strong movement towards a satisfying conclusion.

And the reason for this movement goes back to what's at stake. A stake is a vertical post. Your story is fastened to this stake for support. No matter where the plot goes, the stake anchors it to reality.

Timing

The outline gives you the opportunity to sort out the timing of your story. When exactly does it start and end? What are the seasons? How much time is covered? Signpost the passing of time. You might be planning a dramatic scene in a snow blizzard, when chronologically the story is still in mid-September.

'How old is everyone?'

How old is everyone? Indicate that X is 23, Y 28 and Z 65. As time passes, keep a track of their increasing ages. Babies have a funny way of growing up.

It also surprises me how rarely characters have birthdays. Decide on your characters' birthdays and make them happen, even if in a low key way . . . 'No one sent him a card.'

Historicals and sagas

The matching of a fictional/factual schedule is more complicated if you are writing a book that spans a large or significant historical time period. It helps to set out the fictional outline and historical facts side by side.

On one side put the fictional plotting, then on the other side put the factual episodes, with dates that you want to include or weave into the plot, wars, riots, fires, epidemics. These anchor the story to the historical turn of events at the correct time. Don't forget the changing reigns. Even a servant girl would hear about a king dying and a new one being crowned at Westminster.

Research

The same procedure should be followed for the linking of researched items. Some authors go to immense trouble with their research, put all the information onto index cards, or file and number in clear-leafed folders, some key their research onto a disc. Mark your outline with relevant information where to find your filed or indexed research i.e. Page 477 Peterloo Massacre (Trevelyan).

My research consists mainly of piles of paper on the carpet, on bookcases, on window sills, up the stairs. Don't touch, I know where everything is! My excuse is lack of time.

I do have a system of sorts, using strips of paper to mark pages in books and writing on the top of the paper very clearly what that page contains and the page number. The page number is essential. Bits of paper have a habit of falling out every time you open a book and that page number can save hours of re-reading.

However, for my next book I am resolved to use the clear-leafed folder system. Photocopy the page that contains the researched item, highlight the relevant part in yellow, pop into clear folder.

'Timing and research are crucial for the thriller or crime novel.'

Crime and thrillers

Timing and research are crucial for the thriller or crime novel. It must be historically accurate, even when the past is only yesterday. The research about everything (guns, poisons, medical facts, ferry time-tables, flight times, even bus routes) must be double-checked. Remember and mark where you found the information.

Red herrings and clues should be plotted in your outline, ready for planting in the story. A clue could be too early, or too late; a red herring might never be explained; the disguised clues that a reader might pick up later and think, 'how clever'.

Writers worry about plots. They think every story has already been written. But each writer has a freshness, some new insight or twist. We are each a unique personality. No one else thinks quite the way we do, so use that uniqueness to create something different.

Soon you won't be able to wait to start writing. It'll be an itch you've got to scratch.

The no-outline story

It is perfectly possible to write a story without the aid of an outline and many authors do. Such freedom is exciting because you never really know what is going to happen. But you do have to know where your story is going and the basic theme. The characters need to be strong enough to actually carry the story themselves.

My Jordan Lacey crime series is only loosely outlined because Jordan always seems to take over. She practically writes the story herself. I am merely a useful slave who gets her out of awkward predicaments.

'It'll be an itch you've got to scratch.'

Summing Up

- Check ageing of characters.
- Check passing of seasons.
- Check location of scenes.
- Check travel times.
- Treat: check if your glass needs refilling!

Chapter Four
Crime, TV & Radio, Non-Fiction

A crime synopsis needs different treatment. The basic information is still necessary but cataloguing the progress of the investigation or crime brings another kind of order to the chaos.

This is not the same as a chapter-by-chapter outline, which you may have roughed out to help yourself know where you are. It may fall naturally into chapterish divisions but they do not have to be the same as the chapters in your book.

Think of it as the step-by-step revealing of the clues and twists and turns. And yes, you do have to say whodunnit and reveal the denouement, even if it hurts. An editor wants to know if the story works and the plot is believable.

It doesn't stop you from using a more brilliant idea when you are actually writing. I was on the last page of *Lucifer's Bride*, knew the end, had always known the end right from the beginning, when a new twist suddenly leaped into my mind. It was perfect. I couldn't believe my luck. A great ending handed to me on a plate. Thank you, good angel.

While writing the Jordan Lacey books, I often only have the vaguest idea of who did it. This is because I am writing from her viewpoint, in the first person. Jordan doesn't know so she has to think and be in the same state of uncertainty. Then, I usually surprise myself and make it someone totally different in the last chapter. In *Pray and Die*, it came to me on the last page.

Then one has to go back into the book and make it all fit. The joy of computers.

So let's write a step-by-step synopsis of a crime novel.

Whodunnit?

- 1. The title

- 2. Where is the story set and when?

- 3. Who are the main characters? Briefly identify the sleuth, private or police. Add why is he/she different from the hundreds of others being published.

- 4. What is the crime and who is, or are, the victims?

- 5. Any special circumstances?

- 6. By what means is the crime going to be solved?

Now begin the analysis of the crime investigation, point by point. Number each sentence. Make each sentence brief, just the bare facts. Catalogue each new clue, each red herring, each unexpected development. For example:

> 'Now begin the analysis of the crime investigation, point by point.'

- 1. She finds ex-husband's hidden bank book with recent big withdrawal.

- 2. She discovers he's lent the money to the son of an old friend.

- 3. Husband is shot on street corner and is in a coma.

- 4. The police make her the number 1 suspect. They track a call on her answerphone just before ex-husband is shot.

- 5. She suspects the friend's son is in drug-smuggling trouble.

And so on . . .

This will help sort things out in your mind. You may notice a glaring error; an impossible time fact. Time and distances are always difficult to get right. Check and check again. Use time-tables, maps, a piece of string. Walk it, drive it. Time how long it takes to travel a certain distance. Guessing is not good enough.

A tempting bite

It's important to say whodunnit. The editor wants to know. It may feel dreadful having to give up this closely guarded secret. You may go bananas about your idea getting pinched. There is only the remotest possibility that someone may use your idea, but it is so remote, it's really not worth losing sleep.

I once had a complete short story plagiarised, practically paragraph by paragraph, several years after the original publication of my story. I could only complain to the editor, sending her a photocopy of the first publication (my original story). She was sorry but what could she do about it? Nothing. At least the copy-cat writer lost her reputation.

Children's stories

This is a growing market, yet the National Literacy Trust say that half of children today don't read fiction and that magazines and websites are the most popular material for reading.

Still the publication and sale of children's books continues to soar. The Library Summer Reading Challenge is a great success. It encourages children to read six books in the summer holidays and they then collect all sorts of goodies.

Check that your story is the right length for the age group.

* Picture books – usually 32 pages which are printed in a grid format. Very few words but every word has to count. Submit on A4 paper, indicating page space or a fresh numbered sheet for each page.

* Age 5-6 years - 1,000 words (early readers)

* Age 6-7 years - 1,000-2,000 words (confident readers).

* Age 7-9 years - 2,000-3,000 words (fluent readers).

* Young adults - 10,000 words.

* Teenagers - 20,000-30,000 words

When submitting the shorter books, send the whole manuscript with a brief synopsis of the story. Longer stories should be the usual synopsis and three chapters. Again, if your book has series potential, mention it. Think farms, animals, trains, spooks, mermaids, fairies, Just William, the Famous Five. Suggest further titles.

State the intended age group of the reader.

Writing for children does not mean only using short words. They like the challenge of a longer word. They know the names of most of the dinosaurs. If they don't understand a word, they will skip over it.

Children like to read about someone older than themselves. So a ten-year-old would prefer to read about an eleven- or twelve-year-old. And you do have to read lots of children's books yourself. Take no notice of funny looks on the train.. Most of us have read the Harry Potter books. Moving staircases are my favourite form of transport and all my pictures talk to me.

Radio & TV

If your ambition is to write radio or television drama, then the synopsis becomes even shorter. It becomes a new medium. It becomes the Idea Synopsis.

Producers have no time to read a full fictional-style synopsis, a sit-com treatment or a 50-page finished play. Never send a completed manuscript. You may never see it again. My own 45-minute radio play has been lost in the basement of Broadcasting House for three years.

TV sit-coms

They want a very brief synopsis. The basic idea. Half-a-page at the maximum. It's a tempting bite. Perhaps five or six short, simple sentences. It's an idea synopsis only and a challenge to write. Find a way to make them read it.

Ideally they'd like several ideas to look at. Perhaps five or six. A friend once sent in seventy ideas. A lifetime's work if they liked them all! But only one was chosen for consideration.

Seventy ideas may seem excessive but we have all got more than one idea swimming around. Write them down or they will drown in the swamp of everyday living.

The next step was for my friend to write a five-page treatment of the single chosen storyline. If the producer then liked the treatment, he would give the go-ahead for the writer to complete the whole play or an episode. And that would not be the end by any means; dozens of re-writes during rehearsal might be needed. A re-write a day is not unheard of.

The BBC Writers Room produce helpful guidelines, but update them every few years. The drama slots also keep changing. Keep an eye on the weekly programme details and check that the time length still applies.

If you like the work of a particular producer, you could try sending a one-slot play straight to them. But finding an address is hard. If they have a website, then it's easier to track down an address. Don't expect an immediate answer. They are very busy people.

The idea synopsis

This should contain the three elements, the why, the when, the what. It does not have to be the whole story or even contain the giveaway of the end.

But, like every synopsis, it has to have that grab-all hook. The producer is looking for that something special, something different that catches his attention. Write something you didn't know you knew.

'Write something you didn't know you knew.'

Let's throw together a few ideas. We'll start by:

▧ Saying what slot it is aimed for, radio or TV, and how long.

▧ The title. Sharp, memorable. It may get changed but right now it's *your flag*.

▧ Anything special about the idea.

Here are three Idea Synopses. No prizes for guessing the stories.

1. Split Minds.

    One-hour TV play for 9pm slot.

    Scope for spectacular special effects.

▧ A scientist is experimenting in his laboratory. The experiment gets out of hand and he finds himself turning into a monster. This monster starts to take over more frequently. Somehow the scientist has to get rid of it before it destroys his life and sanity.

2. Glass Princess.

   45 minute radio play for afternoon slot.

   Suitable for children.

   ▪ A scullery maid is badly treated by her stepmother and horrible sisters. A kindly godmother makes it possible for her to go to the royal ball. The prince falls in love with her but she leaves before he can find out who she is. He searches his land with his only clue . . . the glass slipper she left behind.

3. Forbidden Secret.

   One-and-a-half hour TV play for 8pm slot.

   Chilling costume drama.

   ▪ A quiet and shy governess is employed to teach the adopted daughter of a rich and arrogant man. The gothic house is full of strange noises and screams. Someone tries to set fire to the house. The governess hardly dares to believe it when the couple fall in love. But their wedding is halted in the middle of the service when the groom's dreadful secret is exposed.

'Radio is a great potential market. There are hundreds of minutes of air time to be filled every day.'

I have deliberately chosen three well-known stories to show how little of the actual plot needs to be explained in an idea synopsis. It's the idea that has to come across, the essence, the hook, the elusive something that makes it different. Try writing a few famous plots as ideas.

The treatment or storyline, if requested, will then detail the plot and all the spins and swings. A treatment would be about five pages long. After more meetings, more talks and suggestions, it might then be time to write the full episode, the whole play.

Radio is a great potential market. There are hundreds of minutes of air time to be filled every day. New writers and new ideas are welcomed. It gives writers the freedom to go anywhere, be anyone. Who could ask for more?

A proposal for a non-fiction book

Gordon Wells is the expert on writing non-fiction and I suggest you get his excellent book *Writing Non-Fiction Books - The Essential Guide* (Need2Know). He says you have to go out and sell each new idea.

A proposal for a non-fiction book has to have these added elements. A possible publisher needs to know:

- The title - is it catchy?
- Is there a gap in the market for this book?
- How will your book differ from others?
- Does it fit into a current series?
- Who would buy it? Who is the target reader?
- Is the author the right person to write it?
- What are his qualifications?
- Contents of the book, i.e. chapter headings.
- Proposed length, approximate wordage.
- Any proposed illustrations.
- Delivery date.

'Who would buy it? Who is the target reader?'

This information should cover one sheet of A4 paper, single-spacing. It is a brisk, professional and business-like approach. You are both in the business of wanting to sell books and selling something that is practical and marketable.

The non-fiction 'synopsis' is based on the chapter headings. The content of each chapter should be briefly listed. Two pages of single-spacing should be adequate.

If the publisher comes back to you showing interest, he will ask for a sample chapter so that he has an idea of your writing style. And you will have written this while waiting for his reply. Send the very best you've written, unless he specifies a particular one.

It's no use suggesting that you could write a book on hand-making Toby Jugs if you can't prove there are dozens of people out there wanting to buy it and that you are the best Toby Jug maker in the UK. However, if you can quote the existence of Toby Jug clubs, evening classes, even cruise holidays as a source of sales, then you are in with a chance. The hobby market is expanding.

Be truthful about your credentials for writing this book on Toby Jugs. You have to sell your ability, know-how and skill, but if a publisher likes your idea, then you have to go ahead and prove it.

A chapter content might look like this:

Chapter 2: Famous Toby Jugs. Their Value Today. Getting Started. Your Basic Utensils. Necessary Equipment and Materials. Your Design.

'You have to sell your ability, know-how and skill but if a publisher likes your idea, then you have to go ahead and prove it.'

This may not be accurate, but then I know nothing about making Toby Jugs. Remember to enclose an SAE. Who knows? Your idea may be exactly what a publisher wants.

The how-to book

When writing and selling a How-To book, it is essential to get a contract first. Be sure it is going to be published before committing yourself to all that hard work. It is also necessary to assess the competition and make sure that there is a market for your idea.

So look for a yawning gap on the book shelves.

When preparing your proposal, along the lines of the proposal for non-fiction books, your credentials are important, including diplomas and degrees, prizes, papers published, any given lectures.

You might not need a degree to write about *How to Keep Bees* but any How-To book in the health, education or engineering field has to be backed by knowledge and qualifications.

The title must be catchy and say what is between the covers. There are exceptions, of course, and the long title about Ukraine tractors is one. But the tractor title works because it is so weird. Your publisher, when you get one, has the last word on the title so don't be offended if they change it. They know what sells.

And sell yourself and the book in your covering letter. Make it brief but interesting, including all contact details.

Again, don't submit your proposal with any fancy margins, fonts, covers, ring binders, ribbons, buttons or bows. Plain white A4 paper, elastic bands, self-sealing plastic food bag (new) in case your precious manuscript gets dropped in a puddle.

Today's publisher may accept manuscripts by email or CD, which saves any decision-making. Check whether they like submissions by attachment or in the body of an email.

Summing Up

- Be business-like in every aspect.
- Be truthful about your experience.
- Be accurate in assessing the market.
- Convey your enthusiasm for the subject matter.
- Read relevant books.
- Treat: cook an appetising supper. You will need the energy.

Chapter Five
Characterisation

Characterisation is the prime ingredient of any book. Without real characters, everything becomes as sawdust. Even in this book there are two characters, you and me.

Thinking time

When you eventually start to write chapter one, all the initial preparation of planning, plotting and knowing your characters that you have already done will repay dividends. There are lots of mindless jobs, like washing-up and vacuuming, that positively fly by if you are actively engaged in thinking about your story and your characters.

You need that thinking time. Writers who can start from nowhere are to be envied. The rest of us have to plot and plan. I have to think about my theme, my unique idea, the storyline, and most importantly, the characters.

Cardboard characters

You may have a brilliant plot, but if your characters are cardboard then the story will be without life.

If your characters are interesting, believable and well-drawn, you could get away with a plot that is less than riveting.

People want to read about real people, to know what goes on inside their heads, their hearts, behind closed doors. They want to know them *better* than they know their spouses, their friends, their neighbours. We don't really know

'Without real characters, everything becomes as sawdust.'

our friends, what they think or why they do things. We only know what they allow us to see and often that is not much. Do you really know what makes your friends tick?

But a complete characterisation of a person has no secrets from us and therein lies the fascination of reading, and for us, the writing.

Your characters

Characters have an uncanny way of becoming real in our minds. It's surprising and rewarding. They are silent, or not so silent, companions. You might easily 'see' them on a train, the underground, or in a restaurant eating at the next table. You might see your heroine walking a steep butterfly-strewn coastal path, the wind blowing through her hair.

Once I saw my current hero walking along Chancery Lane. Everything about this man was right, the set of his shoulders, even the same purposeful stride. I had to follow him, at a discreet distance, noting every detail about him, pretending that I was going that way as well. Then it got ridiculous and I turned away and resumed my original errand.

'Once I saw my current hero walking along Chancery Lane.'

But the sight of that man was imprinted on my mind. I could always invoke this image when I was writing and it helped to make him a real person.

The next step is to find photographs. I like photographs of my main characters pinned to the corkboard by my desk. It beats wallpaper. But isn't that expecting rather too much? Photographs? After all, characters begin in the mind.

Their photographs do exist. They are around in glossy magazines, newspapers, the Sunday supplements. Look at the advertisements. Collect pictures of:

▦ Faces	▦ Clothes	▦ Houses
▦ Rooms	▦ Furniture	▦ Meals, as served
▦ Cars	▦ Pets	▦ Cities

File under simple headings and keep in files, brown manilla envelopes, plastic folders. You don't have to buy a filing cabinet or start an expensive system.

What you are doing is building up the lifestyle of your characters. They are becoming flesh and blood people with homes, clothes, cars that you can describe with accuracy. Their lifestyle is taking shape. These visual aids are wonderful for creating an authentic atmosphere.

One of my heroines lived in a big room at the top of a watertower, with clover-shaped windows in each wall. It was empty except for an expensive music centre. I would never have thought of this if I had not seen an advertisement showing such a room. I did eventually add a white sofa and a vase of daffodils for dramatic effect. (Also an ancient apple cupboard hidden in a wall.)

The same heroine needed a special long dress for a special occasion. I found a fashion article with the perfect outfit. A top fashion designer had designed a dream gown for my heroine and I borrowed it . . .

As our setting starts to come alive and characters gather their vital statistics, it's time to prepare character charts. It's not enough to know their hair/eye colours, though it is essential to be consistent. Write these two items of information in big letters on a card and prop on your desk.

Changes of eye colour are not unknown in novels. Spotting inconsistencies is sometimes more fun than reading the book. I noticed a change of breed of pet dog in one novel; in another the same door sometimes had a bell and sometimes a knocker.

Character chart

Make a chart for each important character. Fill in the information as and when it comes to you. It won't all come on the same day. Your characters will grow slowly, evolve, as they become real to you. Here are the main headings for the chart. Give each section plenty of room.

Full Name	Age	Height
Eyes	Hair	Style
Scars	Build	Self-image
Health	Occupation	Goals
Positive Traits	Negative Traits	Birthday

- Ambition
- Car
- Favourite Food/ Colour/Clothes
- Type of Humour
- Siblings

- Home
- Hobbies
- Good/Bad Habits
- Parents
- Education

- Finance
- Fears
- Family Background
- Religion

If you fill in half of this chart, then you'll know a sight more than eye and hair colour. Your character is becoming a genuine person, faults and all.

Is this necessary?

The need for this biographical information may not be obvious at first. Possibly the two most important headings are the positive and negative traits of a character. Leave lots of space for these as they will surely grow into comprehensive pen portraits.

'The two most important headings are the positive and negative traits of a character.'

A writer friend asked about birthdays. Surely knowing their age was sufficient? But if a book spans more than a year, then at some time a birthday is going to crop up, even if she dismisses it with a groan and pulls the covers over her head. Even a birthday forgotten is worth a mention. Surely Bridget Jones has a birthday?

It makes life easy if you choose dates that are already familiar or those that are significant to the story.

Full name please. Why not? Most of us have two Christian names and we should know the identity of our character.

It's equally important to know the make of the car that your character drives. Simply getting into a vehicle and driving off is not enough, unless a complete disinterest in things mechanical is part of the character. Their financial situation is also of interest to the reader. We are curious about what people earn or how much they are in debt, the overdraft situation, solvent or not solvent. Don't state exact figures - this dates a book faster than fashion - unless your book is a period piece when a wage of five shillings a week is part of its charm.

Parental background, brothers and sisters, all have a bearing on the formation of your character's personality. Think about your own parents and remember their influence on your life. Were they cruel? Did they ignore their child? Your character is not born in a void, like Superman, floating down to Earth in a bubble.

Knowing your character's favourite foods, clothes and colours is fun. Think about your own life and any part these likes and dislikes play in it. But your character may not care about clothes or food, so not having any interest in such things is what needs to be known.

Favourites

I enjoy giving my heroine a favourite colour and I have a stack of Matchmaker paint charts which give me wonderful shades (saffron, butterscotch, primrose, if she likes yellow).

Hairstyles are interesting, particularly if the style changes with the character's mood or even mid-novel for some reason. Women are prone to using their hair as an outward sign of distress or challenge.

Do they have a mobile phone or not? Or do they hate them? People feel strongly about mobile phones. Are they always forgetting to charge it up?

Bad habits and minor flaws are what make our characters into special people. Sir Lancelot du Lac became all the more believable once he fell hopelessly in love with Guinevere. Eventually, he became a hermit and died alone.

The flaw can be huge or tiny, from an uncontrollable temper, chronic meanness, to something very unimportant, like biting one's nails or never putting the top back on toothpaste.

Knowing your character's health is vital. I am amazed at how many characters in books have perfect health, despite the most harrowing of circumstances. Never a headache or a cold.

We all have fears. We might be afraid of heights, spiders, failure, getting stuck in lifts, being embarrassed in front of friends, saying the wrong thing. Don't we all say the wrong thing sometimes? It's not simply the major fears of death, accident or illness. ('I'm not afraid of dying; I just don't want to be around when it happens'. Woody Allen.) It's the small fears of life which make our characters real.

'Bad habits and minor flaws are what make our characters into special people.'

Are you beginning to see why a Character Chart can be such a help? It'll save time in the long run if you are 100% sure that your hero does not take sugar every time he begins to stir his coffee.

Summing Up

- Make a character chart.
- Let your characters grow with time.
- Find their photographs from magazines.
- Find photographs of settings.
- Treat: a mint every time you add a new fact.

Chapter Six

Titles & Other Firsts

The first of several firsts is the title. Next in importance comes the opening paragraph, then the first page and the first chapter. They are your book proposal; they sell it.

The title

The title is like a headline that declares the image of your story. So find a stylish title. It should contain the essence of your book. Invent a title that makes it stand out from the hundreds of other titles on the bookshelves at WHSmith. Such a lot depends on your title. Sometimes they come to you in a blinding flash and you know that it's instantly right.

The title is the first of the firsts that has got to grab an editor or publisher. She'll be keener to carry on reading your book if it has a good title, a fascinating opening, a page-turning first chapter.

A title should have rhythm and be easy to say and remember, as well as telling the reader what the book is about and what they can expect to read. If you buy a glitzy airport paperback called *Brocade*, you know instantly that it isn't a handbook on dressmaking. Clothes may feature in it, but not the nitty-gritty of cutting, tacking, and how to put in a zip.

Apparently, people love it when the consonants M, K, G and P are used for initial words in a title. *The Eagle has Landed* managed without them, so has *The Day of the Jackal*.

But let's think how important titles are with their imagery and suggestion of plot. Do you think these titles would have become bestsellers?

Scarlett's Southern Adventures

'The title is like a headline that declares the image of your story.'

Father Ralph and Obsessive Ambition

A Burnt Flyer in the Desert

Gabriel Oak and Bathsheba

Tips for Household Management

Lilliput's Unusual Prisoner

Rhythm

There is a fashion for one-word titles at the moment but, two-word titles have more rhythm and stay in the mind. Words with two or three syllables have a kind of flow . . . *Virgin Soldiers, Whisky Galore, Eastern Approaches, Peter Abelard, Bridget Jones's Diary*. Each of these titles makes an announcement.

The title should come from within your book; the story itself often suggests one to you, or you suddenly see it already written in the text. *Gone with the Wind* is taken from the text and was only found after a long search by Margaret Mitchell and her publisher.

'Two word titles have more rhythm and stay in the mind.'

If you become stuck over a title and it's holding you up, then:

- Give it a *brief* working title.

- Hand the problem to your unconscious.

- Try lists.

A working title

Sometimes I feel I can't even start a book or a short story because it doesn't have the right title. This can hold me up for weeks while I search through the Bible, the *Dictionary of Quotations and Proverbs*, the racing pages. Horses have amazing names . . .*Titch Wizard, Tactical Mission, Timeless Times, Gone Savage, Crystal Jack* . . . and that's only from today's newspaper.

Quotations are another brilliant source for titles and the quiz game Catchphrase on television. Page-turning through the *Dictionary of Quotations and Proverbs* always suggests titles that you long to use.

60

Open at random. Page 316. Immediately I find: *Burning Daylight; Angels Wooing; Farewell Goes Out Sighing; The Speaking Foot; Mine Oyster; Chance or Death* . . . all from *The Merry Wives of Windsor* and Troilus and Cressida (Shakespeare). None appropriate for this book (wait, *Burning Daylight* might be an alternative to *Midnight Oil*?)

Making lists is another way of finding a title. I found the title *The Secret Taj* by this method. Make three separate lists of single words. The first list is of strong nouns that have a prominence in the story; the second list is of adjectives that also have relevance; the third list contains the mysterious element of the theme. Cross-line them from one list to another, any way, any order, stirring the words. Titles come from all directions. Then suddenly, from the crossed lines, the right one appeared . . . *The Secret Taj*.

Our unconscious works while we are asleep. It's nice to think that our other self is beavering away while we are unwrinkling our faces. Twice I have presented my unconscious with a title problem, and twice the perfect title has popped into my mind some days later when I wasn't thinking about it at all.

For my crime story I wanted a title from the Marriage Service but all the best phrases had already been used . . . Dearly Beloved, To Have and To Hold, Till Death Us Do Part.

I had written the book, revised and revised, polished every word and printed it out. The manuscript was ready to go to my agent, but it wasn't going anywhere without a good title.

That night, before going to sleep, I explained the dilemma to my unconscious. Three days later, as I was walking through Victoria Station, a title popped into mind. It was complete, perfect . . . *Lucifer's Bride*. A bride fit for a fallen archangel, the devil himself.

> 'It's nice to think that our other self is beavering away while we are unwrinkling our faces.'

The hook

The opening paragraph must contain a hook of some kind to grab the reader's interest, a special something that holds her attention in its crab-like claws. This paragraph should signal some information that gives the reader a clue as to the content of the book.

The first page of your proposal chapter is equally important. It's what makes a reader buy the book. Watch people at the bookshops when they pick up a book. This is what they do:

- Read the title, glance at the cover and author's name.

- Turn it over and read the blurb on the back cover.

- Flick through the book to see if they like the distribution of black and white (i.e. whether it's all narrative or all dialogue or an acceptable mixture of both.)

- If interested, they open the first page and read the first few paragraphs.

If the first paragraphs are boring, the transaction will probably go no further. Back goes the book on the shelf. A sale is often as simple as that.

It is usually on those four pieces of information that a reader decides whether to buy a book or not. Since few authors have any control over the cover or the blurb, then it's up to us to make the title and the opening paragraph the very best possible.

'It is usually on those four pieces of information that a reader decides whether to buy a book or not.'

The opening paragraph has several functions. It should, if possible, show the main character in action, hint at what is to come, set the tone of the story, promise the reader that the strands of the plot are going to collide. A tall order for one paragraph.

My own favourite opening paragraph is from Mary Stewart's *Touch Not the Cat*:

'My lover came to me on the last night in April, with a message and a warning that sent me home to him.'

Note the weird contradiction . . . her lover came to her in the night and yet he can't possibly be there because she says she has to go home to him! A message and a warning.

There are nine styles of opening paragraph which are frequently used:

1. Weather forecasts.

2. Moment of change.

3. Shock, horror.

4. Dialogue.

5. Scenic.

6. Lo and Behold.

7. Mysterious.

8. Action.

9. Introspective.

Here are a few quick examples, not from published novels, but just to illustrate the styles:

1. 'It was raining hard. Rain flooded the pavements and sent the shoppers hurrying for shelter; the gutters were overflowing with a flotilla of sodden debris.' There is nothing wrong with that opening as a picture of a wet shopping street. But where's the hook? How about adding four words 'and sent all but one of the shoppers hurrying for shelter' . . . immediately you think, why, who?

2. 'She took the new baby into her arms. Life would never be the same. Now she had to work and think for two, and she would do that, even though the baby was not hers. But she was going to make it hers.' (Plenty there.)

3. 'The guillotine fell with a sickening thud . . . it was too late for justice.'

4. ''I'm not staying,' he said, flinging open the door. 'And I don't care if you're dying. Don't expect me to come to the funeral.''

5. 'The Yorkshire moors rolled into misty distance, timeless and intriguing, their secrets hidden in dells and valleys and guarded by the small streams that burbled innocently between the rocks.' Add one word . . . barely hidden and there's a new dimension.

6. 'Time waited in the wings, as it had for centuries, relentlessly watching the players.'

7. I can't improve on Mary Stewart's opening paragraph. Read it again and see how clever it is.

8. 'He climbed the wall steathily, the knife hidden in the sleeve of his leather jacket. He had exactly two and a half minutes in which to find his target and get out.' (Ticking clock)

9. 'The lone woman stood at the end of the harbour, watching the ferry leave for France. She wondered if she would have the strength to walk away; no one knew how much it had cost her to be there in the first place.'

The first page

The first page should contain three promises:

- That there is going to be an intriguing or memorable situation.
- Indicate who are the main characters.
- Set the tone for the novel so that the reader knows whether she is in for a romance, a thriller, a sexy shopping saga, science fiction or adventure.

The first page is a contract with the reader. I, the author, promise you, the reader, this kind of story.

It should be written and re-written until it is right.

Romance

This genre demands that the heroine is introduced straight away. Even on the first page there is going to be something about her that intrigues us and we are about to get a strong hint of the basic conflict ahead.

Here are the first two paragraphs of my book *Daughter of Tor*:

> She tugged at the sash of the old-fashioned window and threw it open, letting the sea wind cool her overheated brow. Troy was angry. Grace was making her give up her home and it was not fair.
>
> 'I'm having to move out, lock, stock and bottles of good French wine, at two day's notice. Can you believe it, tree? And all because of a man.'

Look how much we can learn from those few lines. The heroine's name is Troy. She lives by the sea. She is fond of her home. She is lively and spirited, has a good sense of humour. The conflict is already planted because Grace is making her move out - for the sake of some man, a total stranger. It is obvious that the man is going to play an important part in Troy's life and the story.

And she's talking to a tree! This lady is certainly different. All of this in two paragraphs.

Mainstream/crime/murder

For these genres, we want more of the setting. We need to see, touch, smell, be in the place where the story starts. We want to feel the atmosphere, whether it's a sleepy, drowsy village, a dynamic and powerful business, a bustling city, a steamy foreign location. Each of these clichés conjures up a stereotype place but it's then that the writer, with the writer's style and imagination imprint the setting with a uniqueness.

The reader needs to know fairly soon if it's the kind of murder story with a sleuth, amateur or professional. Now the canvas is much broader and as well as the hooks, it gives information, begins the story with some intriguing situation or thought.

These are the opening paragraphs of *Lucifer's Bride*:

> When Adele Kimberley meticulously planned her elder daughter's wedding, she was hoping it would be the wedding of the year. And that's exactly what it became. The wedding of the year.
>
> She did not know that the tin cans would never clatter down the drive, the carnival streamers never stream and the vintage car, despite its effortless battalion horsepower speed, would not be going anywhere.

From this we learn three important things: that the wedding goes seriously wrong; that Adele and family are well-off and she is ambitious - wedding of the year, a drive outside the house, a vintage car - there's a hint of imminent disaster, of coming notoriety. There's also another daughter. Quite a lot of information in two paragraphs.

Instant story

The fashion for a slow, leisurely beginning with a long description of a place, the weather, or some family background has gone. There is not the time nor the market for leisurely starts. Readers want to be into the story right away. They want instant story.

'Now the canvas is much broader and as well as the hooks, it gives information, begins the story with some intriguing situation or thought.'

Chapter One

The first chapter is the pivot of the whole story. It's no use chapter five being wonderful; no one will reach it if chapter one is not exciting, intriguing, and arouses our interest or curiosity. Who is going to wade through four chapters to get to the best one, fifty pages on? Not the publisher's reader.

This chapter will be full of information for the reader.

- Set the tone of the book and tell the reader whether the story is going to be a romance, crime, science fiction etc.

- Introduce your main characters by name, showing them as vital and interesting. Describe their looks briefly, but also show their personality, good and weak traits, making them real people.

- Establish the setting, the atmosphere, letting the reader identify with this fictional world.

- Indicate the coming conflict, the main problem, intrigue, mystery, crime, romance, action. Plant clues as to what is going to happen.

Summing Up

- A brilliant, eye-catching title.
- An intriguing first paragraph.
- A first chapter sets the tone.
- Plant clues.
- Treat: relax with your favourite music.

Chapter Seven

Beating Writer's Block

Some writers never get writer's block. For others, it is an ever-present monster, prowling round the fringes of their mind, setting traps that they fall into every time.

A colleague of mine says the answer is a double whisky. There are many writers who find alcohol loosens the creative juices. Alcohol for them is the oil that makes the motor run smoothly. They don't have writer's block, just creaking joints.

There are three categories of writer's block and degrees of self-help which can banish them long enough for your confidence to return:

- Daily reluctance to start writing.
- Problems in storyline.
- Total loss of creative ability.

The first is only temporary, self-inflicted, and can be treated with a certain degree of light-heartedness and tolerance. We all hate starting work, the actual nitty-gritty of making ourselves sit down and begin the process of writing. Some writers have rituals before they can get going - like sharpening their pencils, tidying their desk. I can't even find my desk - it's somewhere under all that paper.

Let's look at ways of getting started. It helps to begin work at the same time each day, every day. My time is 10am which gives me a chance to do an hour's frantic housework, but I drop the dead duster on the stroke of ten.

'There are three categories of writer's block and degrees of self-help which can banish them long enough for your confidence to return.'

Under starter's orders

- Make a cup of coffee.
- Switch on word processor or uncover typewriter.

- Put in memory stick or sheet of typing paper.
- Read what you wrote yesterday.

Reading what you last wrote is the crucial key. Read yourself into your current work by going over yesterday's writing. You will find yourself unconsciously editing, improving, adding a word or two and by the time your coffee has cooled, you'll be back in harness.

Of course, it isn't always as easy as this. If you are stumped and unable to get going, some warm-ups could help . . .

- Write nonsense.
- Write about the weather.
- Write some dialogue with your main characters in a new situation.

Write anything that comes into your head. Thoughts and ideas will start flowing from outer space.

Nonsense writing is just a run in for the day - like revving the engine before you let off the handbrake - and can be deleted later. It serves a purpose.

Writing about the weather is the same kind of exercise, but it need not be deleted if it usefully sets the scene in a story. The British are obsessed by the weather. We all want to know what's happening to our erratic climate. Snow in April. Heatwaves in November. Try to write something magical, let your imagination take off.

A kind of exercise

Inventing a totally new situation and making your characters talk about it can bring a stale story to life. Choose a simple scene: they are at a bus stop waiting for a bus. Your characters will take over, talk, argue, snap at each other . . . perhaps they'll suddenly say something you'd never expected and that's exciting.

Leave that situation and go back to your storyline with your characters very much alive and talking to each other and doing things.

Much later, delete the fake bus stop situation. It was only a device to wake up your characters.

Dead ends and cul-de-sacs

This is a more serious block, not just the morning hiccup. You may be depressed by rejections and the fear of failing. Your favourite editor may have left. Your story has ground to a halt and you are left worried and in despair.

Firstly, don't panic. We all have doubts about our ability to ever write again or the worth of what we are writing. Take some time off, perhaps a few days. Walk, read, swim . . . be active as well as leisurely. Writing is a sedentary occupation (unless like Hemmingway, you write standing up) and some physical activity will give you a inner glow. Be kind to yourself, pretend you are convalescing from an obscure non-threatening illness.

Sometimes we write ourselves to a standstill and deserve a break. A brisk walk along a cliff top or a wave-lashed shingle beach will blow away stuffy writer's blues. A weekend in Cumbria, walking and climbing, letting the endless views heal a tired mind . . . a writer's course where you talk shop with like-minded people and collect loads of sympathy.

Notice things when you're walking . . . an ant carrying a leaf almost as large as itself . . . the roots of a tree, centuries old, distorted by the October 1987 storm . . . the sudden breathtaking beauty of a kestrel hovering in a clear sky.

Walk the dog, walk the cat, walk the budgie. Walking and reading are the ailing writer's remedies.

When you return to your desk, refreshed and hungry to start work again, re-read your previous chapters. If nothing happens, then you need to go back to the drawing board and find out where you are going wrong. Ask yourself these questions:

- Do I really know my characters?
- Have I enough plot to sustain my story?
- Is the motivation of my characters truly thought through?
- Am I writing the right book?

> 'We all have doubts about our ability to ever write again or the worth of what we are writing.'

■ Do I really care about this book and care about the characters?

If the honest answer to this last question is *no*, then you are writing the wrong book and no amount of re-working is going to help. Put it away and start something new. Look through your notebook of ideas and see what really excites you.

If the answer is *yes*, then perhaps you have cut corners on your homework and you don't really know enough about your characters and their motivation for doing things. Maybe the storyline is thin.

So write a character sketch of your main characters. If you come to a halt after a simple physical description, then you don't know them.

The 'what-if?' game

'They stimulate the imagination, provide stepping stones in a new direction.'

Play the *what-if?* game with your plot. Come up with at least ten alternative *what-if?* ideas, the wilder the better. They stimulate the imagination, provide stepping stones in a new direction.

The *what-if?* game is a form of lateral thinking, thoughts going along different routes. The situation could be the morning after a disastrous date. Setting: heroine in her kitchen. Begin with simple, low-key *what-if?* ideas, such as:

■ She makes a cup of coffee.

■ She falls over the cat.

■ She drops the coffee and scalds herself.

■ He phones and leaves a message.

■ There's an accident outside and she rushes out thinking it's him.

■ A friend phones, saying she's seen him throwing suitcases in his car and driving off at speed.

■ She sees a newsflash on television that two ferries have collided.

■ She hurries to find him but her car won't start.

■ A gas main explodes in the street.

Pretty wild? Inventing a whole group of new alternatives gives you two sets of decisions to make: those which you throw out instantly as being unsuitable and those which have possibilities if re-worked in another way. Your brain is working again. Perhaps your plot needs a change in direction.

You could decide to use two of your *what-if?* ideas - maybe dropping the cup of coffee and the newsflash - inserting the information that he was going to travel by ferry that day earlier into the story. Now we have a situation, not merely a disastrous date.

Black depression

There is no way of being light-hearted about total, mind-blowing writer's block. For a writer, this is a devastating nightmare. The light of life has gone out. What is there left to do in the darkness?

I have never experienced this and I hope I never will. Writing is my obsession, the joy of my life, my passion, and without it, I really don't know how I would live. I suppose I would give a home to several more cats, watch mindless television and shrivel inside like a forgotten apple.

Emotional trauma of some kind is usually the cause of complete writer's block . . . bereavement, divorce, an accident, ill health. All these things need time to get over and this is what you must give yourself. Time, my friend. Do not despair. Life is always changing and it will change again. Sometimes a field must lie fallow.

'Life is always changing and it will change again. Sometimes a field must lie fallow.'

A therapy

But many writers find that writing is a therapy in difficult situations.

A friend of mine came home from her husband's funeral and wrote a short story that afternoon. It did not mean she was not upset or a callous woman; she knew that writing would help her. Writing was her solace.

The daughter of another writer was in a terrible accident. Fiction writing was impossible. This writer had been commissioned to write a true fact book and keeping that December 31st deadline was her lifeline. Being professional she made herself keep it. She wrote so much each month and no more. The rest of the year was devoted to nursing her daughter. The book was delivered on time.

But what if you can't reorganise your life to take in this new situation and your mind has closed itself to writing? Like pain, I would say . . . relax, go with it. Accept the block, don't fight it. This is your fallow time.

What do fallow fields do? Absolutely nothing. Don't take on more guilt if a blank and dusty screen sits idle on your desk. Dust the screen and put some flowers on your desk instead.

Fallow fields gather up nutrients. Read everything in sight. What bliss to have the time to read and read, the sheer luxury of it.

Do the things you've always wanted to do but never had the time . . . go to stately homes, go on a coach tour and look at gardens, go to the theatre, the cinema, horse racing. Seek out museums in small market towns; look at places in England you've never seen. This country has hundreds of villages, teeming with history, all worth visiting and exploring. Keep in touch with your writing friends and go to weekend conferences, even if you are not writing. At least they will understand how you are feeling.

One day there will be a stirring inside you, like the very first crack in the ice. The thought will come that you want to write again, but now, after so long, you are terrified.

Terrified of failure. We all feel that fear at times. You need a linguistic inhaler.

A stream of consciousness

Take the Dorothy Brande treatment once a day, preferably first thing in the morning, with a cup of tea. She says, in her wonderful book for writers, that writing something, anything, in a notebook after waking from sleep, is the best way to start the day.

'Fallow fields gather up nutrients. Read everything in sight. What bliss to have the time to read and read, the sheer luxury of it.'

Keep a notebook by the side of your bed and write a few lines every morning. No one is going to see what you write, random thoughts, night dreams, day dreams, descriptions, vent your anger, despair, your grief.

When you feel like it . . . no hurry . . . get out a dog-eared manuscript that was abandoned years ago. You are not going to make yourself write. You are going to re-type it. Your editing mind will automatically take over, a word here, a word there, a scrap of dialogue brought up to date. You might even enjoy what you are doing . . . after all, it's only typing.

Write small things at first. A poem. Perhaps only eight lines or haiku, the Japanese verse form in 17 syllables. They are so compelling. No one is going to see those lines straight from the heart, funny, nostalgic, poignant. Put them away with your dreams.

Play around with ideas for a very short story. Eight hundred words can't bite you. What does it matter if you bin it? And what was that idea you had for a novel, that marvellous twist ending you never used?

By now the fallow field will be bursting with the promise of new growth and the paralysis will have gone. And with it the ogre of writer's block. Banished to the dark forest.

The slough of despair

Make a list of what gets in the way: lack of time, no ideas, feelings of failure, feeling foolish and embarrassed, back ache, hunger, thirst, tiredness, don't know any writers, publishers, agents. This is a list of anxiety and self-doubt. Assure yourself that it is often the most gifted who suffer such torments.

If you are still stuck, then let's break the spell with relaxed writing. Here are some writing topics. They are different but could easily fill twenty minutes of writing.

- What is the longest time you have ever gone without sleep?

- What was the most difficult phone call you have ever made?

- Who would you like to interview? What would you say?

- Can you remember a vivid dream?

- How about a vivid childhood memory? (I remember running away . . .)
- Live a day in someone else's skin.
- Write today's horoscope for yourself or another person you know.
- What was the worst meal you have ever had?
- What was the best meal you have ever had?
- That celebrity interview – re-write it from his point of view, him describing you.

You have been writing in a relaxed state without the monster of Anxiety. Monsters go off duty on a train, on a beach, on a headland. This relaxed writing state can be summoned. It's a state in which you gain confidence, ability and freedom.

Writing is the second most exciting activity invented for humans. Eventually it could become your first. Christy Brown – *My Left Foot* – wrote five novels with only his little left toe.

Summing Up

- Read and edit yesterday's work.
- Go for a walk.
- Retype an old manuscript.
- Write a stream of words on waking.
- Read a good book.
- Treat: a bar of Fairtrade dark chocolate.

Chapter Eight

The Joy Of Polishing

Now is the time to become craftsmen and show the skill of our technique.

Polishing means honing words to diamond-sharp perfection. Cut, weigh, hone and polish. Treat every phrase as a precious stone which has to be polished to a brilliant sparkle. Some people call it revision, but polishing sounds more positive.

To hone also means to yearn, pine, moan or grieve, and there's a lot of that going on when it's necessary to cut and cut again. As we re-read our work, we yearn to have written better, pine for lost inspiration, moan as we spot lapses and mistakes, grieve as we have to ruthlessly hack at a well-written line that does not add to the story.

Each word, phrase, sentence, paragraph, has to be judged and weighed for its contribution to the prose. If found wanting, then it should be replaced by something better or cut completely. Judicious pruning never hurt a rose bush.

I enjoy the process of polishing. The hard graft of putting down a mass of words from scratch is over. In the summer the garden beckons and I can sit with a chapter on my knee and work it over and over again, thinking about each word, sentence by sentence, the balance of dialogue and narrative.

> 'Treat every phrase as a precious stone which has to be polished to a brilliant sparkle.'

Deciding when to polish

When the arduous work of the first draft is finished, polishing - once a housework-type word - is now your first concern. For months you have been stimulated to write this fascinating story and you have let it run . . . and run. It is with immense pride that you type 'The End' and reach for a large gin and tonic or the remote control.

Take time off. It's necessary to let your manuscript cool and settle into shape. You wouldn't cut a cake straight from the oven while it was hot. You deserve a breathing space before beginning second draft re-writing.

A breathing space

Some authors never touch a word once it is written. There was an articulate fairy at their christenings and her name was Confidence. They send off their manuscript straight from the word processor, no tampering, no tinkering; word-perfect from day one. The rest of us have to work and work hard to achieve what we hope is our very best.

Leave your short story for a few weeks, longer for a novel. You need to create an intellectual distance. Start something else, walk the dog, feed the family, invent a new filing system. It's ideal to have a planned holiday as your self-imposed deadline for finishing that work on time.

'You need to create an intellectual distance.'

Of course, while on your break, you're making notes. All writers are compulsive note-takers. Never move more than a few yards from your house without a small notebook and a pen. I once posted a letter to a friend with scribbles on the back. She phoned me up. 'What's all this gibberish on the envelope?' she wanted to know. I had thought of a great line of dialogue on the way to the postbox and had to write it down.

In this cooling off period, it's useful to jot down anything that you want to check for your book:

- Check weather at the wedding.
- Have I been consistent about time of service?
- Find out how fuse works . . .
- What happens to the dog?

Don't start tinkering. Anxious tinkering can ruin what is a perfectly acceptable first draft. Fiction fatigue often sets in after long, sustained effort and the mind is in no fit state to make rash decisions.

80

Editorial revision

This is another kind of revision. If an editor at a publishing house likes your manuscript, she may suggest some changes. Perhaps she thinks there should be more dialogue or more about the growing relationship between the hero and heroine. She may think that the background distracts from the plot and needs toning down.

Professional writers, after an initial panic, and a few days digesting the editor's letter, comply with these suggestions. They want to get their book published.

Go along with these revisions, and make them to the best of your ability. This is the attitude of a professional writer. If there is some aspect that really goes against the grain to change, then it's best to have a talk with the editor and see if some compromise can be reached.

While making editorial revisions, keep a list of page changes and briefly what has been rewritten. For example: Page 7 - more dialogue. Make a list. If the rewritten work creates an extra page, it's acceptable to number it '7A' without having to renumber the entire book. It helps the editor when she reads the revised manuscript if she can locate new work immediately. She has probably read dozens of other books since looking at yours, and she'll appreciate a quick guide.

If an editor thinks that a marketable book can be made better, she'll enjoy working with a writer who listens, co-operates and can translate those suggestions into skilful writing. It could be the beginning of a successful partnership.

'Professional writers, after an initial panic, and a few days digesting the editor's letter, comply with these suggestions.'

Choices

Polishing has its own creative excitement, although it is essentially about choice and selection. There are four basic requirements:

- Cut and polish.
- Invent.
- Add.
- Check.

Cutting

The object of cutting is to tighten the prose, being ruthlessly self-critical. Look upon it as eliminating the flab.

Cut absolutely everything that has nothing to do with your story. But cut wisely. Don't hack, mangle, tear out the roots or you won't have anything left.

Sometimes whole scenes have to go or an entire character removed from a scene . . . a superfluous secretary, an intrusive waiter.

Cutting for required length is equally hard - but should be part of your initial planning. Always keep a running check on the word length of each chapter.

Polishing

'Always keep a running check on the word length of each chapter.'

It becomes a kind of sixth sense. You know what you are doing without having to use a check list. The more you polish, the more it becomes second nature:

- Cut for length.
- Cut unnecessary adjectives, adverbs.
- Cut superfluous words.
- Tighten phrases.
- Check length of paragraphs.
- Smoothness of paragraph transitions.
- Use more evocative words.

My own pattern of working is to revise the previous day's work on disc briefly each morning, before starting on new writing. This is kind of 'reading and writing in' process is invaluable.

I revise again, in longhand, when the first draft is printed out and I can see how it looks on a page, and then much later, honing and honing fine details to the ninth degree before the final print out of each page.

Inventing

Maybe your book needs new scenes, new dialogue, new twists to the tale, even exposition. Exposition is like explanation, the writing that is the least like action, more information or a viewpoint. Extra research can be inserted, but not much. Research should be like an iceberg - only one third showing.

Perhaps in your mad rush to get the first draft down, you left out a whole chunk of story which, it's now painfully obvious, must be there or the plot doesn't make sense. Start writing again, but now it is far less of a chore because that awkward scene has the scaffolding of the rest of the story to hold it up.

Strengthening

This is putting flesh on the bones of your plot, filling out your characters into real people. You knew it had to be done sometime, but were in too much of a hurry to do it earlier because you wanted to get on. The story has started talking back to you, telling you what it needs, and you're making a mental note, or better still, making lists on a sheet of cardboard propped on your desk.

1. From this new emotional distance you see lots of things that can be brought out, buried information that your unconscious had slotted in the story for you to discover.
    In the first draft of my crime story, *Lucifer's Bride*, I discovered red herrings I didn't realise I had planted (sorry about the mixed metaphor); an added motive which became an explosive new twist. They improved the story and they had been there all the time, waiting to be noticed.

2. Make strong scenes stronger with extra lines of dialogue, more powerful verbs, vigorous action, dynamic thoughts. This is your chance to strengthen an undeveloped scene that wobbles on the page.

3. By the end of the first draft you'll know your characters pretty well, so find ways of fleshing them out so that the reader will know them as intimately as you. Thoughts will come to you naturally as you go through each page.

'Research should be like an iceberg - only one third showing.'

4. This distancing makes it possible to see patterns emerging. Echoes, circles, mirrors of things that happened earlier, happening again, making satisfactory ripples. You're cleverer than you thought you were. You were actually too close to see it happening at first. Now these patterns can be focused and the echoes made more vibrant, the mirrors more accurate, the circles complete. Patterns are essential. They are the framework of completeness.

5. Your best writing is often done at this later stage. There's time for that considered thought, searching for exactly the right phrase, the right word, an original simile. You are not in quite such a rush.

Knowing what has to be done is a slow learning process. But since it is a draft we are working on, it doesn't matter how many times we cross out and try a new phrase, something more intriguing.

Dialogue

'Patterns are
essential.
They are the
framework of
completeness.'

While economy is the key to good dialogue, avoid writing it in a kind of verbal shorthand. The reverse is also true. In real life, we ramble, waffle on, talk in half-finished sentences. All this has to be tidied up or cut out.

The principal functions of dialogue are:

- To convey the character of our story actors.
- To convey any necessary information that advances the plot.
- To show the emotional state of the speaker in this scene.

A rhythm

Dialogue should have a rhythm. If a line of dialogue does not sound right, try saying it out loud. Real dialogue is peppered with repetition, long pauses and tautology. Tautology is the use of words merely repeating a meaning already conveyed. If this realism creeps into your fictional dialogue, cut it out. Write what seems natural, but keep it crisp and short. There isn't room for irrelevancies. And watch out for over-long sentences. We don't talk in paragraphs.

Repetition

It is only too easy to repeat words and phrases, even similar situations keep popping up. The same adjectives and adverbs can pepper our prose without our noticing first time around. Roget's Thesaurus is the writer's best friend. Learn how to use this wonderful book. Put in on your Christmas list.

Repeating the name of a character too often is another weakness that can be tidied up. Use 'he' or 'she' if it's clear who is present. In an exchange of dialogue between two characters, their names can be edited out completely. It might be necessary to insert a short sentence of thought or action, just to remind the reader who is speaking.

Clarity and accuracy

This is an opportunity for getting rid of forests of dead-wood padding. Time to correct inaccurate facts, inconsistencies, lapses of memory. Writers sometimes introduce pets which never get fed or taken for walks, change makes of cars mid-story, send a heroine to the library on a Sunday, state the obvious . . . 'he crawled on all fours.'

Maximum curiosity

Many writers in the throes of crafting a novel forget the value of producing a page-turner. It's worth looking once more at the opening and ending of every chapter. Every chapter should end with some line of drama, revelation and intrigue that make the reader continue reading instead of putting out the light.

When she does turn over the page, the beginning of the next chapter should not disappoint her with a dull or formal beginning. You've planted a bait at the end of the previous chapter, now re-hook your reader with the beginning of the next.

Give your manuscript an elegance and eloquence. Hone it into shape and remember that spaces can speak.

> 'Every chapter should end with some line of drama, revelation and intrigue that make the reader continue reading instead of putting out the light.'

Summing Up

- Let the manuscript cool off.
- Check opening of every chapter.
- Check closing of every chapter.
- Hone, whittle and polish.
- Treat: this hard work deserves a meal at your favourite restaurant to unwind.

Chapter Nine

The Long-Distance Writer

Writing is not a compartment of life, it is a whole existence. If you don't write, then you are not a writer. Writers write every day.

A day without writing is a lost day, never to be recovered; a day to mourn. Write anything - 1,000 words, 500, 100, your journal. Write when you first wake, any rambling phrases that come into your head. Let the thoughts flow down your arm and onto the paper.

Sometimes this unconscious writing will make sense. Sometimes lovely, out-of-context phrases appear. Keep them safe. They may come in useful.

Loneliness

The loneliness of the long-distance writer is undisputed. It is a solitary occupation, shut away in your ivory tower for hour after hour with only your thoughts and the winking eye of the cursor for company.

Yet you are not truly alone because of all the people in your head and the ones you are creating on paper. They are your other world. The real loneliness comes from not being understood. Non-writers do not understand what you need. They may not appreciate that you are desperate for time to yourself, peace and quiet, no trivial interruptions, but most important of all, that you need to be taken seriously.

Writers become isolated, wrapping themselves in a thermal suit of armour to prevent the barbs of relationships and the community penetrating their vulnerability. They withdraw from a world that is often hostile to their profession.

Ernie Wise got it right when he protected his writer's fragile image with wild exaggeration: 'Yes, I wrote four plays this morning. Another five in the afternoon'.

'Writing is not a compartment of life, it is a whole existence.'

So when my daughter (with kindness in her heart) asks me what I've done today, instead of saying that I wrestled with two hopelessly inadequate pages, I'm far more likely to say: 'Wrote a book on the train, two short stories over coffee, planned a saga while waiting for a bus.'

This turns my serious obsession into a joke, but allows me to get on with my writing.

For years I was a closet writer, despite being published. I knew from experience that I lost friends if I told them that I wrote. A glassy look would come into their eyes as if I had suddenly grown an extra ear; they stopped being natural and were wary of what they said in case they were being 'put into a book'.

How could I reassure them that I don't put real people into my books; that I have enough characters in my head for a hundred stories? Certainly a lot of facts are stored in my mental filing cabinet, but then they are stirred around with a spoonful of time and a pinch of imagination and reappear in a totally different guise.

'If you really want to write, you'll find the time.'

Now I don't tell anyone what I'm doing - except my writing friends. I joined the Romantic Novelists' Association, the Crime Writers' Association and the London Writers' Circle; conferences and courses at Swanwick in Derbyshire, and Earnley in Sussex, were a revelation . . . hearing first-class lectures, shop-talk and making friends.

My advice is to keep your writing to yourself. Resist the temptation to chat with friends. Save talking till you are with fellow writers.

Shortage of time

We are all short of time. Long-term time (life itself) and short-term time (this week). It's the familiar wail of writers; some are genuine and some are using it as an excuse for not writing.

'I've been far too busy to write.' 'It's been hectic at the office.' 'Don't know where the time's gone.' What they really mean is that writing is not their first priority. If you really want to write, you'll find the time.

Planning and pacing

There is free time in every day, if you look for it. And this applies if you work full-time or part-time at a bread and butter job as well as write. If you are a full-time writer, then planning and pacing your day is essential.

But for those who combine another occupation with writing, as well as running a household and bringing up children, time is as scarce as rain in the Sahara. It's easy to say get up earlier - 6am is a beautiful time of day when the world is fresh and quiet and you seem to have all the air to yourself. I do this if I'm nearing a deadline and this extra hour in the morning is beyond price.

I worked on the train like Trollope, commuting to London, writing longhand in a notebook, then typing it onto disc in the evening. This transfer was, in fact, its first revision. Weekends were earmarked for solid writing, morning, afternoon and evening, with only time off for a lightning strike at the shops and a swim at our leisure pool.

Even the busiest mother should be able to find time for herself in the day, perhaps odd half hours when the children are napping. She should call this time her own and forget the ironing. I've typed with two toddlers sitting on my lap, both jamming the keys with sticky fingers; now I'm more likely to have a Persian cat on my lap with the other cats reorganising the filing in a highly individual manner.

'You have to be ruthless, make time, be selfish.'

You have to be ruthless, make time, be selfish. No one is going to say to you: 'Would you like this afternoon off for your writing, dear?'

Relationships

Juggling the roles of mother, wife, lover, husband, and breadwinner with being a writer is a hard act to maintain. You keep dropping the balls.

A non-writing partner is going to find it difficult to accept that you enjoy shutting yourself away with these imaginery people. He/she is likely to feel jealous, particularly if you are writing a romance and your hero is one dishy man. Non-writers get aggrieved by the amount of time writers need to spend alone. They think that it reflects some kind of failure on their part.

Reassure your partner that these ficticious (use that word a lot) people, although very alive to you, are nothing like as good as the real thing. Sometimes writing a love scene can spill over into real life which can use up a lot of calories.

Ask for help

Ask for help in the research, especially if you know nothing about cars or mechanical details. Include your partner in research trips even if you do lag behind with a notebook in your hand. Share your successes with the family. Celebrate with a meal out, a theatre trip, a holiday, depending on the size of your success. Share everything with them, except your writing time . . . and the storyline.

Don't tell your family the plot until it is in first draft. They can kill it off faster than a Parliamentary guillotine with a few well chosen words. Keep the magic to yourself. Talking about a story dissipates that magic. Why write it if you've already told everyone?

'Talking about a story dissipates that magic.'

If your partner is also a writer, then I should imagine the problems are rather different, ie nobody makes supper. But his and hers word processors could be fun . . . and talking way into the night . . . having a companion that is compatible. Many writing partnerships seem to flourish, as long as they are not competing in the same field.

Children are easier to train, just remember to feed them regularly. They quite like having a mother who keeps out of their way and disappears for hours with an ancient typewriter, now computer. Mine were born into a writing atmosphere. They have never known anything different. They can always interrupt me especially if they bring a cup of tea. They spent their childhood charging down to the library to count how many times my books had been borrowed.

'Forty-three times this year, Mum!'

God bless the Public Lending Right and all who work at the Registry.

Discipline

So there's a lack of time, a stroppy partner and nowhere to write; you could be forgiven for giving up. Self-discipline is your sword.

It would be easy to forget the whole thing, switch on the telly and start knitting. No one needs to know that the cover hasn't been off your word processor for weeks, dust welding the pages of your thesaurus. You need three firm disciplines:

- A definite start time.
- A daily quota.
- A realistic deadline.

Starter's orders

If you are at home all day give yourself a starting time, like an office. Be at your desk promptly. On the dot. Punch your card.

If you are a part-timer, then perhaps 8pm is your time to clock-in. Eight till eleven . . . three productive hours. Work five weekdays and that's fifteen hours. Two pages an hour (I'm slow) and that's thirty pages in a week . . . 300 words a page and that's roughly 9,000 words. Keep this up for two months and you've written a book.

Trollope set himself a daily quota of words to write and kept a strict check on his output. I keep a daily record in a work diary. Every working day I write down how many pages I've written, revised or printed. Any day off is recorded (sick/conference/research). Several blank days for no good reason reproach me and I am guilt-ridden.

My four lectures on The Ninety-Day Novel makes this crystal clear.

'Keep this up for two months and you've written a book.'

Daily quota

Set yourself a realistic target each day. Two thousand words a day was too high for me and I couldn't reach it regularly. It made me feel a failure. Now my daily target is 1,000 (3-4 pages) which I can reach and often exceed if the writing is going well.

Another prolific novelist has a weekly target of 15,000 words. Pretty high. But it does even out the good days and the bad days. She always takes the whole of Sunday off. She needs one complete day to recuperate mentally and devote to her family.

A deadline

'This kind of deadline sharpens the mind considerably.'

Impose a deadline for your work. Tell yourself that your draft/revision/complete manuscritp must be finished by Christmas/your holiday/when visitors descend. This kind of deadline sharpens the mind considerably.

If you have been commissioned to write a book, then you will already have a contractual deadline which you should strive to meet. Fingers crossed that you'll stay fit, find the stamina and there are no family disasters.

If you don't meet your personal deadline, perhaps it was unrealistic. You can't write an airport brick in slim book time. I set deadlines before a holiday or conference, so that I can go off with a clear conscience and have a good time.

Somewhere to write

The kitchen table is not ideal. All that clearing away and ketchup on pages. But it's better than nothing. A book-lined study with a panoramic view is beyond the hope of most writers. My desk looks worked on; it has immense character somewhere beneath an Everest of paper.

Aim for a table or desk where you can leave out your work. If you have to put everything away, you'll never get started again. The sheer labour involved will sap your strength.

Need2Know

Work in a nice area. A pleasant room. Why should you be banished to share a cramped box room with broken tennis racquets or the far corner of a draughty, cheerless passage, like an unwanted ghost? Perhaps a table could be installed in the dining room or main bedroom with a bookcase for reference books and current files. Files stack flat on a bookshelf. Have a pottery jug for your pens, a pretty coaster for your coffee mug.

I work on a large dining table in the furthest corner of the dining room. There are two windows which look out onto the garden and a Japanese maple tree. Birds feed from the nut bags; cats stalk the birds, crouched on branches; sometimes it's hung with washing. The russet colour is warm and forever moving. It lives and breathes.

There are four bookcases at my side and two cork pin-boards on the wall for notes and pictures. Recently box files and folders of research, maps, stationery and carbon copies were moved upstairs to a tiny sewing room to cut down on the 'office' type clutter. So now I have an office upstairs and a writing desk downstairs. I am no longer surrounded by old research and cuttings.

Conferences

Conferences are invaluable. They stimulate and refill the well of ideas if it has run dry. A conference glowing keeps the juices flowing. They are held in all parts of the country, some a long weekend, others six days to a week. Look in writers' magazines for announcements and send off for an application form. They get filled quickly and are value for money.

Creative writing classes

Enrolling for a local creative writing class is a sensible route of tuition for the beginner. Writing is a craft which can be learned and classes help you to avoid amateurish mistakes.

One disadvantage is that the set classwork might be such fun that you never have time to do your own writing. Don't let set work take up all your creative time.

And check the writing credentials of the writing tutors. Discover what they have really had published. Some tutors are less than honest with the truth.

'They stimulate and refill the well of ideas if it has run dry.'

My First Monday Club is now in its fifth year. We meet the first Monday of the month which gives its members three weeks and six days to do some writing. They are a talented lot and it's wonderful at each meeting to hear of stories now published and prizes won or short-listed.

Correspondence courses

This checking credentials also applies to correspondence courses. Some people find written criticism of their work very helpful, but that keeping up with a heavy course load leaves them with little energy for any other writing.

Such courses and classes are addictive. A perpetual student is simply putting off the day when he becomes a professional writer.

There are many excellent How-To books available and a library of them on your bookshelves is an ideal way of getting started. They are instant stimulation.

Summing Up

- Create your own time and pace.
- Find your own writing space.
- Involve the family.
- Meet other writers.
- Treat: watch a good television drama and learn from it.

Chapter Ten

The Book Proposal

There are three basic elements to your book proposal. Get them together and you are ready to submit your work:

- Covering letter.
- Synopsis.
- The first two or three chapters.

You have written or nearly completed your book, making sure the first couple of chapters are brilliant. The synopsis is brief, perfect, sparkling. No more writing, checking or re-writing. All that is left to do is the covering letter. Those few paragraphs are equally important.

The covering letter is a fanfare, a trumpet call, muted but neverthless it says: 'This is me. Here I am. This is how I am. Read me.'

It should have:

- Legibility.
- Clarity.
- Briefness.
- Quality.

1. Use plain, good quality writing paper. I saw one covering letter written on a torn out page from a shorthand notebook. The scrap of paper spoke louder than the scribble of words on it.

2. No gimmicks, borders, crossed quills, logos, fancy computer graphics. The editor will not be impressed. It looks as if the author has time to play around on his word processor instead of writing.

'The covering letter is a fanfare, a trumpet call, muted but neverthless it says: "This is me. Here I am. This is how I am. Read me."'

3. Choose the publisher carefully. Check that he publishes your kind of book. The same if you are approaching an agent. Check that the agent represents crime, romance, science fiction, whatever you have written. Some agents only want an initial letter in the first instance. If so, keep your book proposal until they ask to see it.

4. Phone up the publisher or agent and get a name to write to. Begin formally: Dear Ms Smith. Don't use her Christian name unless you know her.

5. State simply what you are enclosing, using the *title* of your book.

6. The second paragraph should be one line about the type of book and its theme, repeating *title*.

7. The third paragraph should give your track record, if you have one. Make it brief. Don't say that your aunt loves the book or that it won second prize at your writers' circle.

And that's all. Don't forget to sign clearly, enclose return postage, add your telephone number and email address.

'Don't staple, punch holes or tag.'

Nothing fancy

Do not pack your proposal in a fancy ring binder or cover. Don't staple, punch holes or tag. Collect, stack, put an elastic band sideways round, and another longways and pop into a clear plastic bag. Freezer bags are sturdy and don't split. Label with *title* and your name/address. The covering letter should be uppermost so that it is the first item seen. Send in a bubble-pack Jiffy bag, clearly addressed.

Check that you have enclosed everything, especially sufficient return postage, then fasten securely and post. Use the Recorded Delivery system if you're feeling nervous.

The wrong covering letter

Dear Madam Editor

I do hope you don't mind my sending you this novel. I feel it is exactly right for your list as you have published many like it.

I am a completely new writer so please forgive any mistakes. I should be very grateful for any criticism and helpful advice. My local writers' circle think it is great but I am sure that it could do with professional help.

Perhaps you could phone me. I am available any evening after six o'clock. I look forward to hearing from you.

Yours sincerely

Miss S Bloggs

PS The title of the book is *Forever Sinning*

This covering letter is going nowhere and I'm sure you can see why.

The right covering letter

Dear Ms Smith

I enclose for your consideration a synopsis and the first two chapters of a 100,000 word novel called *Forever Sinning*.

Forever Sinning is the story of four friends who take the pop world by storm but come to grief along the way.

Forever Sinning is my third book. The other two were published by Green & Green. Sufficient stamps are enclosed for return of the ms when you have reached a decision.

All good wishes,

Yours sincerely

Stella Bloggs

Celebrations

It's time to celebrate. You have achieved a lot, climbed a mountain by writing a whole book and nearly finished polishing the manuscript. You've also written a synopsis and covering letter and you have put it all together to make a professional book proposal. It stands a good chance when it reaches its destination because it has all the hallmarks of a competent writer.

You deserve some time off to wine, dine, walk and talk. But not too long. There are those last few chapters to be polished, so that all is ready if the publisher comes back saying he wants to see the completed manuscript immediately.

Surely there is another manuscript waiting to be written or research to be started? Don't extend your holiday time. Stay in writing-mode. It's a wonderful feeling. Never let it slip away. Writing is a gift for the few.

'You have achieved a lot, climbed a mountain by writing a whole book.'

Summing Up

- Keep your covering letter short.
- Don't waffle.
- Use good quality paper.
- No fancy packing.
- Put on correct postage.
- Treat: celebrate!

Need2Know

Glossary

Like all crafts, writing has its trade words. Here is a glossary of writers' jargon. Now you'll understand what everyone is talking about.

Acronym
Word formed from the initial letters of other words or syllables, i.e. AKA, WRAF, NATO.

Active Voice
There are two ways of writing a statement, in the active voice or in the passive voice. The active voice is more effective because it's simple and natural.
They turned off the television. *Active.*
The television was turned off. *Passive.*
Jane made some tea. *Active.*
The tea was made by Jane. *Passive.*
Sometimes use of the passive voice is right, say - the windscreen was shattered by a stone . . . the windscreen having more importance than the stone in this sentence.

Advance
This is money paid to you by a publisher in advance of your own possible earnings. You do not have to return it if your book royalties don't reach that amount. New writers usually accept the suggested advance with gratitude; established bestsellers ask for more.

AKA
A weird word coined by list-makers, abbreviating 'also known as' for when writers use more than one name.

Antagonist
This is the character in opposition to your main characters, the troublemaker, the catalyst; can be a person or a group.

Background
This is the situation or setting where you choose to bring your characters to life, whether it be a hospital, a business, a particular country or city.

Back Story

This is what has happened to your characters before you began your story.

Blurb

On the back of a book cover you'll find a few paragraphs which tell you what the book is about. This is known as the blurb.

Category Romance

This is a small-sized paperback novel with a set number of pages (usually 186-188) and a set length of 50,000 to 55,000 words. 'A compact jewel' is how one American author describes this genre.

Clichés

Clichés are expressions and situations which have become trite from overuse. There are a few acceptable ones but the rest should be avoided. Clichés come easily to mind when writing. They can be used in dialogue because it's our natural way of speaking. Most writers try to think of a different way of saying the same thing.

There are cliché people too (the tart with a heart of gold, the eccentric professor) and cliche situations (the triangle, the misunderstanding, the overheard remark).

Deadline

The date by which your manuscript is due if you are contracted to a publisher. Be reliable. Your personal deadline is an aid to disciplined writing.

Eponym

This is a word coined from a person's name, i.e. sandwich, wellington, hoover, mackintosh.

FBSR

First British Serial Rights are offered by the author when a short story or feature is sent to a magazine. This means that the magazine can publish the story/feature once only. If you are a new writer, you might let the World Rights go. Selling Foreign Rights of published work is not easy unless you have an agent or foreign agent.

Flashback

A flashback is a scene from the past which is sometimes necessary to show a character's motivation or explain what happened previously. It should be used sparingly in a book.

Formula
Category romances have basic happy-ending plots. This is called formula writing. The publishers still want originality and fresh ideas.

Frontspiece
This is the first page of your ms, unnumbered, with title, your name, address and approximate number of words.

Galley Proofs
Galley proofs are the page proofs which your publisher sends to you for correction. They are unbound, loose, on thin paper. Their purpose is for you to correct mistakes, yours and the typesetter's, not a last opportunity for re-writing. Alterations cost money. There's a list of the proofreading marks in the *Writers' & Artists' Year Book*. The latest technology produces print perfect pages.

Genre
This refers to the types of popular fiction published. There's romance, westerns, science fiction, spy stories, adventures, crime, thrillers.

Glossies
Expensive magazines printed on good quality paper.

Gothics
Atmospheric stories, often centred around large gloomy houses with the heroine in great danger.

Graphology
The study of writing systems, the use of punctuation, capital letters, hyphens etc. Also the study of handwriting.

Introspection
A character's unspoken thoughts.

ISBN

The International Standard Book Numbering is what it says, a numbering system for all published books. Publishers get the ISBN from The International Standard Book Numbering Agency Ltd, 12 Dyott Street, London, WC1A 1DF. It is not a legal requirement. There is no charge.

Metaphor

The comparison of one object to another by the transference of meaning, implying a resemblance. For example: 'He was a lion in battle.'

Minimum Terms Agreement

MTA champions a fair deal for authors. At least seven publishers have signed and their contracts are an immense improvement on the old chaos.

Mixed Metaphor

Metaphors together which are incongruous, ie 'Without beating about the bush, he took off like a scalded cat.' The politicans' favourite: 'With our shoulders to the wheel, we'll keep the flag flying.'

Narrative

Relating events, telling a story as if you (the author) were that person, linking material between dialogue.

Outline

This is a writer's working guide, a practical chapter by chapter breakdown of main scenes and events in the story and the development of the plot.

Pace

Pace carries the momentum of the plot. Long sentences slow things down. Short sentences add action, tension, suspense, immediacy. Stories need both.

Padding

Unnecessary padding is overwriting. Too many words trying to say too little become boring and irrelevant. A padded book is a boring book.

Partial

Publishers like to see a partial rather than the whole manuscript. A partial is the first two or three chapters with a synopsis, a brief covering letter and return postage.

Plot

A plot is the story or plan of events arranged in sequence with a form of development. Good plotting is planning a story ahead.

PLR
The Public Lending Right is the payment to authors from public funds, proportionate to the number of times that a book is lent out from selected libraries during the previous year.

Print Run
This is the number of copies printed of a book.

Protagonist
This is an ungainly word meaning the principal character in your story. It comes from the Greek, meaning the first actor.

Pruning
Cutting with precision.

Pulps
Cheaper magazines printed on poor quality paper.

Reader Identification
The reader should be able to put him/herself in the shoes of the hero/heroine and understand their motivation, sympathise with them, be living their story.

Remainder
All the books left over when a publisher decides that a title has run out of steam. He sells them off, well below marked price, to cut-price bookshops. Writers rush to snap up the bargains.

Royalties
This is the percentage of the retail price which the publisher agrees to pay you. It will be in your contract. The average is 10% for hardback but it could be 2% or 3% on big sales of cheaper paperbacks. If it's based on net receipts, then the rate should be higher. The statements (and the cheque if sales have overtaken the advance) come twice a year.

Saga
A long novel covering several generations or a period of years in a family.

Self-Publishing

This is totally different to Vanity Publishing. You do every step of it yourself. Find the right printers, and it can be rewarding. But, be warned, it is hard work. Then you have to sell your book.

Semantics

This is the study of the meaning of words.

Short Forms

The short form of words used constantly: sd, wld, shd, abt, appx, etc, used when making notes or writing in longhand. Send me a good one for 'the'.

'Show Not Tell'

This is probably the hardest concept of writing to grasp, but simply means that a good writer shows what his characters are thinking and feeling, rather than telling the reader. Instead of making the plain statement that 'John is cold', let John show how cold he is by what he says, does, or thinks.

Simile

The comparison of two unlike objects using 'like' or 'as' as joining words. 'He ran like the wind.' The lake was as still as glass. 'She was as sleepy as a cat.'

Slant

To slant a story is when you write a story to meet the specific requirements of a magazine or publishing house.

StoryLine

The storyline is the plot of a book, film, play; what happens next, then next again, the thread upon which everything hangs.

Style

Style is simply the individual way you write, the unique you, your voice, your tone, especially how you use words. The way you write sets the tone of the book. Your command of the English language, your choice of words, your interpretation of life is your style.

You may have several different styles: one for novels, one for short stories, or one for genre romances and a different, faster pace for thrillers.

Style is the essential you that will shine through your writing. It is as much part of you as your fingerprints or DNA.

Synopsis

Once more, a synopsis is a short, informative narrative covering the major content of a book, which is used to sell the work to an editor.

Syntax

This is the construction of a sentence and the grammatical arrangement of words in a sentence. We unconsciously absorb this knowledge from reading well-written books.

Tag

This is a device giving a character some kind of personal label which sets him apart - a swagger, a loud laugh, a hat, a phrase. Watch characters in television series for ideas.

Tearsheets

These are the pages containing your story or feature that you tear out of a magazine. You may want to sell the foreign rights or send them as examples of your work to an editor.

Theme

Most books have a theme, even if you don't realise it. It's a statement about life and people, a universal truth that comes from the drama and conflict in the story. Love conquers all, faith works miracles, brothers under the skin (cliches) are obvious ones. This premise should be summed up in one sentence.

Tip Sheets

Many magazines give away guidelines as to what kind of stories they are looking for. These are updated as lengths and requirements change.

Transition

A sentence or two that moves the story on by linking scenes.

Vanity Publishing

This is when an author pays a publisher for the production of his book. It is not to be recommended and is often very expensive. Never pay for publication unless you are a millionaire. If you are a millionaire with money to spare, why not start a new publishing company . . .?

Viewpoint

There are two viewpoints for telling your story. You can tell it in the first person, which is the single viewpoint, using the pronoun 'I' all the time. The third person construction allows viewpoint from several different characters and 'he' and 'she' are used.

Voice

There is Active Voice and Passive Voice (see above) and also the Omniscient Voice of the author. This is the author talking like God, the allseeing and knowing being. Sometimes it's known as the Narrative Voice.

Word Count

A wise writer counts words. Most writers work out the average number of words per line (usually about ten to twelve) and the number of lines per page (probably 25) and multiply. This would give an average of 250 or more words per page. Some word processors have a word count, but most publishers need to calculate white space as well. One word of dialogue on a line would still count as ten, and not one, because when it's printed it will take up a whole line.

Writer's Block

This is not a guillotine for failed publishers. It describes the situation when a writer gets stuck, when an empty page or screen stares at them and they cannot think of a single word to write. A period of despair.

Writer's Cramp

This is a muscular spasm caused by prolonged writing. It can be caused by gripping a pen in a certain way or hitting the space bar on a typewriter with ferocity. Your keyboard touch should be lighter, though it's hard for a traditional typist to learn not to thump. Writer's cramp for keyboard users is more likely to appear in the form of backache or neck stiffness. Make sure your chair is the right height and your angle of viewing the screen is five-degrees downwards. And move frequently. Get up and walk about. A soft roll of foam in front of your keyboard, to support your wrist, can help alleviate any pain. I use an unwanted shoulder pad.

Help List

Here are some addresses which may help you:

Public Lending Right

The Registrar, PLR Office, Richard House, Sorbonne Close, Stockton-on-Tees, TS17 6DA.

The rate per loan has increased for the first time in three years to 6.29 pence. Data was collected from 912 library branches.

If you are inspired, 250 authors got the maximum payment of £6,600. The next layer down went to 362 authors and 364 the one below that. The lowest level was paid out to 17,280 authors. There were 14,188 nil payment authors.

Don't forget to register when your book is published. Make a note of the ISBN. Your book must be registered by 30th June of the current year to qualify for payment. Write to them for an application form. Payment is made the following January.

Writers News and Writing Magazine

Warners Group Publications plc, 5th floor, 31-32 Park Row, Leeds, LS1 5JD UK
Editor: Jonathan Telfer
Subscriptions: Collette Dimbleby   Email: writersnews@warnersgroup.co.uk
These are both excellent monthly magazines and full of useful information. Writers News is by subscription only and well worth the quarterly payment. Writers Magazine is then sent to you free. It is also available at WHSmith and other bookshops and newsagents.

Reference Books

Writers' & Artists' Yearbook (A & C Black)
The Writers' Handback (Macmillan)
Roget's Thesaurus is a must
The Guide to Book Publishers (Writers' Bookshop)

The Writers' Handbook is enormously helpful. It is more informal and contains specific information.

Writers' Organisations

Crime Writers' Association

Membership Secretary: Christine Poulson, Padley Mill, Upper Padley, Grindleford, Hope Valley, S32 2JA Tel: 01433 630480.
www.thecwa.co.uk
membership@thecwa.co.uk

Romantic Novelists' Association

Enquiries: Nicola Cornick, Highcroft, Church Place, Rodborough, Stroud, Glos GL5 3NF Tel: 01453 750544
www.rna-uk.org
ncornick@madasafish.com

Society of Authors

84 Drayton Gardens, London SW10 9SB
Tel: 0171-373 6642

Writers' Conferences

Writers' Conferences are not for teaching you how to write but they are immensely valuable for networking and meeting other writers. And you learn a lot from the top lecturers and varied courses.

South Eastern Writers' Conference

Weekend in Spring at Bulphan, Essex. Contact: Marion Hough, 47 Sunningdale Avenue, Leigh-on-Sea, Essex, SS9 1JY Tel: 01702 477083

Southern Writers' Conference (known as Earnley)

An excellent weekend in early June, at Earnley Concourse, nr Bracklesham Bay, Sussex.
Contact: Lucia White, Stable House, Home Farm, Coldharbour Lane, Dorking, Surrey, RH4 3JG Tel: 01306 876202

The Writers' Holiday (known as Caerleon)

Week-long in July, more leisure-orientated.
Contact: Anne Hobbs, 30 Pant Road, Newport, Gwent, NP9 5PR
Tel: 01633 854976

The Writers' Holiday (known as Caerleon)

Week-long in July, more leisure-orientated.
Contact: Anne Hobbs, 30 Pant Road, Newport, Gwent, NP9 5PR
Tel: 01633 854976

There are many more courses, conferences and weekends in different parts of the country listed in the various writing magazines, but I am only mentioning the ones which I can personally recommend. Apply early, go along and have fun.